W9-CDY-743

ALEX'S TABLE

Library of Congress Cataloging-in-Publication Data available.

ISBN 978-0-9857768-1-7

Printed in the United States of America.

♥

We would like to dedicate this book

to the thousands of families

affected by childhood cancer.

Together, we will find a cure.

Coach
Musser
Alex's
Lemonade
Stand

Look throughout the book for these special icons:

H - Recipe is from a childhood cancer hero, hero family or researchers

K - Recipe is kid-friendly or easy for kids to help make!

CONTENTS

Photo Collage (pages 10-11): Thank you to The Loomer Family, The Musser Family, The Smith Family, The Batton Family, The Porrata-Powell Family and the Heywood Family.

WHEN OUR DAUGHTER ALEXANDRA "ALEX" SCOTT TOLD US SHE WANTED TO HOST A LEMONADE STAND, WE NEVER IMAGINED HER FRONT YARD LEMONADE STAND WOULD GROW INTO A MOVEMENT TO CURE CHILDHOOD CANCER.

The key to Alex's efforts to help children with cancer has always been her belief that everyone can contribute to the cause. Alex knew that she could not help other children alone—she needed her family, friends, doctors, businesses and supporters from all over to join together. Today, through Alex's Lemonade Stand Foundation, her legacy continues to inspire and bring together families, companies, schools, researchers and individuals who are passionate about helping children with cancer. This cookbook is another example of how that legacy has inspired so many to act on those passions and come together – in this case through food and cooking.

So, we bring you *Alex's Table*, a place where everyone is invited to share in the legacy of hope for cures for all children with cancer. *Alex's Table* represents our willingness to all come together, raise a glass of ice cold lemonade and then dig right in to finding cures. Inside, there are over 50 recipes from world-class chefs, childhood cancer researchers, ALSF supporters and childhood cancer families. Every participant has donated their talent and recipe to create this beautiful book and we hope you agree that the result is something special.

We welcome you to Alex's Table and thank you for sharing in our daughter's legacy, one recipe at a time.

Liz & Jay

LIZ & JAY SCOTT
Alex's Mom and Dad
Co-Executive Directors, Alex's Lemonade Stand Foundation

FOREWORD

Some people spend their time on earth, maybe more than 70 years, attempting to leave a meaningful legacy to their family and the world. Some are successful, many are not. Imagine existing on this planet only eight years, but in that short period of time, making a difference and continuing to leave a legacy 12 years after the fact. Alexandra "Alex" Scott accomplished that and so much more.

Alex spent her life battling cancer. Although she was wise beyond her years, her generosity and good will towards others superseded everything. She raised a million dollars for childhood cancer her last year of life, and her energy and everlasting spirit continue to this day.

Alex's Lemonade Stand Foundation, now a global charity, has brought people together for several years, raising money and keeping her memory alive. Through the help of hundreds of the best chefs in the world at culinary events such as The Great Chefs Event in Philadelphia, L.A. Loves Alex's Lemonade, Lemon: NYC and Lemon: Chicago, people have eaten extraordinary food, visited with friends, bid on fabulous auction items and, in the process helped kids with cancer.

Think about it. Every family, especially during holidays such as Christmas, Thanksgiving, Easter, Passover or on a Sunday afternoon in the middle of summer, love to congregate in the kitchen. Maybe they assemble in the backyard around a barbecue, reminiscing about days gone by and thinking about the future of kids and grandkids. Whatever the case may be, friends, family and food go hand in hand.

Chefs, perhaps the most generous group of humans ever put on this planet, have given their time, their talent and now their recipes, all in the name of Alex Scott. We hope you make many of these amazing dishes and share them with others. And when you do, take a moment to look up in the sky, give a special thank you to Alex and let her know how grateful you are for everything she accomplished.

MARC SUMMERS

Proud member of the Board of Directors for Alex's Lemonade Stand Foundation
Host of The Food Network's "Unwrapped" and "Ultimate Recipe Showdown"

MAIN COURSES

Tuna Tagliata with Fennel and Orange

MARC VETRI

A note from Chef Vetri: Tagliata (tahl-ee-atta) means "sliced" in Italian and trattorias often serve tagliata di manzo for lunch, a thinly sliced rib-eye steak served on a bed of arugula. Here, I have some fun with the whole idea of "sliced." Instead of beef, I use fish. Instead of slicing the fish like a steak, I pound it thin into one big slice. Instead of arugula, I serve it with fennel that has been cut into thin strips. Even the oranges are segmented to give you only the sweetness of the orange and none of the bitters of the membrane.

SERVES 4

4 ahi tuna steaks, about 5 oz each
⅔ cup plus 3 Tbsp extra virgin olive oil
2 Tbsp fresh rosemary leaves, torn
1 fennel bulb
2 seedless oranges
Salt and freshly ground pepper
1 Tbsp chopped fresh flat-leaf parsley

Put the tuna between sheets of plastic and pound to a ½" thickness with a heavy pan or the flat side of a meat pounder. Put the fish in a Ziploc plastic bag with the ⅔ cup olive oil and the rosemary and marinate in the refrigerator for 4 to 6 hours.

Trim the stems about 1" off the top of the fennel bulb. Thinly shave the fennel into ⅛" thick half-moons. The easiest way is to use a mandoline slicer, even an inexpensive hand-held model, and pass the trimmed stem end of the fennel bulb gently and repeatedly over the blade. Discard the core, dark green parts and tough root end or outer layers of the bulb. You should end up with about 2 cups of fennel strips.

Segment the oranges into supremes (remove membrane from the fruit and cut into slices), working over a bowl to catch the juice. Measure out 1 Tbsp of the juice, pour it into the bowl and drink or reserve the rest. Gradually whisk the remaining 3 Tbsp olive oil into the juice slow and steady until blended. Taste and season lightly with salt and pepper. Add the fennel and oranges, taste and season again with salt and pepper and let stand at room temperature until the grill heats up.

When the grill is hot, scrape the grill rack clean and oil it with an oily paper towel. Grill the tuna on one side only, creating cross-hatch marks on that side. The easiest way is to look at your grill as if it were a clock and start the tuna pointing toward 10 o'clock. Grill until marked, 1 to 2 minutes, then point the steaks to 2 o'clock and grill until cross-marked. Use a wide metal spatula to flip the tuna onto plates so the grilled side is up.

Arrange the salad over the tuna, drizzling on some of the vinaigrette. Garnish with parsley.

Reprinted with permission from Rustic Italian Food *by Marc Vetri.*

CHEF MARC VETRI is the chef/founder of Philadelphia's critically acclaimed **Vetri Family Restaurants**. In 1998, he and business partner, Jeff Benjamin, opened the eponymous, fine-dining restaurant, **Vetri**, in Philadelphia to universal acclaim. Within two years of the restaurant's debut, he was named one of *Food & Wine's* "Best New Chefs" and received the *Philadelphia Inquirer's* highest restaurant rating. In 2005, he was given the James Beard Foundation Award for "Best Chef: Mid-Atlantic." Following years of continued success at Vetri, Marc launched **Osteria**, **Amis**, **Alla Spina**, **Pizzeria Vetri** and **Lo Spiedo**. In 2015, Urban Outfitters Inc., a leading lifestyle specialty retail company, acquired several of the Vetri Family restaurants including Amis, Osteria, Pizzeria Vetri, Alla Spina and Lo Spiedo. Following the acquisition, Marc and his partner Jeff Benjamin began managing URBN's food and beverage operations as well as working with URBN to expand the Pizzeria Vetri concept nationwide.

Marc is the author of *Il Viaggio di Vetri*, a collection of more than 125 of Vetri's most-requested dishes. His second cookbook, *Rustic Italian Food*, brought artisan cooking into home kitchens and was named one of the top cookbooks of 2011 by such outlets as *Bon Appétit*, *St. Petersburg Times* and *The Huffington Post*. He most recently released *Mastering Pasta* in 2015. In addition to his cookbooks, Marc's writing can be found on *The Huffington Post* where he is a regular blogger.

In addition to his storied career in the kitchen, Marc is also the driving force behind the Vetri Community Partnership, a non-profit organization whose mission is to empower children and families through fresh food, hands-on experiences and education. Marc and Jeff Benjamin are the co-founders of The Great Chefs Event in Philadelphia which brings together scores of the country's greatest chefs to raise money and awareness for Alex's Lemonade Stand Foundation and the Vetri Community Partnership. The Great Chefs Event has raised millions of dollars for childhood cancer research since its first event in 2006.

Grilled Country Ribs with Watermelon, Green Coriander and Cilantro

PAUL KAHAN

A note from Chef Kahan: Alex's Lemonade Stand Foundation is a charity I was introduced to by my good friend Marc Vetri. The fact that the money raised translates directly to research and saving lives is something that my business partner, Donnie Madia, and I have been very enthusiastic about since the beginning. Yearly, One Off Hospitality Group supports ALSF in Philadelphia, New York, Los Angeles and now in Chicago.

I was introduced to the Pork Country Rib recipe by my good pal Jason Monroe and his wife Diana at a BBQ that my wife and I threw yearly for the staffs of our restaurants. When we were planning the menu for The Publican, a customized version seemed like a no-brainer. It's been a staple on our menu ever since. Lip-smacking good!

SERVES 3 TO 4

To make the grilled ribs:

3 lb of country-style pork ribs
1 Tbsp sambal
½ cup palm sugar
4 sprigs of cilantro, stems & leaves
½ onion, sliced
2" ginger root, peeled and minced
6 garlic cloves, minced
½ cup thin soy
3 scallions, thinly sliced
¼ cup rice wine vinegar
1 tsp black pepper
1 Tbsp sesame oil
2 Tbsp Chinese mustard

Combine all ingredients except for the mustard.

Marinate the ribs the morning you plan to cook them (6 to 8 hours ahead) by first rubbing each rib with the mustard and then covering the ribs with the marinade.

Light a charcoal grill and let the coals burn to embers.

Remove the ribs from the marinade and save the marinade.

Char grill each rib for approximately 5 minutes per side or until medium well.

(continued)

Dunk each rib back into the marinade and continue grilling for an additional minute per side. This technique enhances the charred flavor.

To make the marinated watermelon:

½ seedless watermelon cut into 1" cubes
Juice of 2 limes
¼ cup extra virgin olive oil
Salt and pepper to taste

Before cooking the country ribs, in a large mixing bowl, combine all the ingredients and let macerate in the fridge for 30 minutes to an hour.

To make the coriander vinaigrette:

1 tsp toasted coriander seeds
1 small shallot, diced
4 Tbsp champagne vinegar
½ cup extra virgin olive oil
1 tsp honey
Salt and pepper to taste

In a small sauté pan, toast coriander seeds over low heat for 2 to 3 minutes until the seeds become fragrant or begin to pop. Pour seeds onto a cookie sheet and crush slightly with the back of a cool sauté pan. Place coriander, shallots and vinegar in a small bowl for 5 minutes. Whisk in the olive oil and honey and finish with salt and pepper.

To prepare the tomatoes:

1 qt cherry tomatoes
Salt and pepper

Wash tomatoes under cool water and slice in half.

To assemble the ribs:

Plate ribs. Mix cherry tomatoes with coriander vinaigrette. Top ribs with marinated watermelon. Pour and scatter the tomatoes over the top of the ribs and watermelon.

CHEF PAUL KAHAN has become the nationally recognizable face of Chicago chefs. Passionately seasonal, unconventionally creative and dedicated to the inspiration of classical cuisine, Kahan has received international acclaim for **Blackbird**, **avec**, **The Publican**, **Big Star**, **Publican Quality Meats**, **Nico Osteria**, **Dove's Luncheonette** and most recently **Publican Quality Bread**. Awarded "Outstanding Chef" by the James Beard Foundation in 2013 and "Best Chef: Midwest" in 2004, Kahan has earned the praise of many who claim him to be one of America's most influential working chefs.

In 1999, shortly after Blackbird opened, *Food & Wine* placed Kahan on their "Best New Chefs" list, recognizing his highly individual approach to cooking and the talent that Chicago diners have celebrated for years. Despite accolades and adoration, Kahan's biggest accomplishment remains his work as a mentor for young chefs. Kahan is a strong supporter of Alex's Lemonade Stand Foundation for childhood cancer research, as well as Pilot Light, an organization dedicated to enhancing schoolchildren's perception of food through hands-on education. Paul is partner chef and co-host with Donnie Madia for Lemon: Chicago. Paul is a devoted husband to his wife Mary, an ardent music lover and bike aficionado.

Angel Hair Pasta with Caviar and Lemon

ALEX GUARNASCHELLI

A note from Chef Guarnaschelli: Domestic caviar is something that can be had for a good price, and only a small amount is needed to make a statement. Whenever I do buy it (which is admittedly rare), I find myself almost at a loss for how to honor it with an unusual preparation. Let's face it: straight out of the little glass jar on toasted bread with a schmear of crème fraîche is a great way to go. I also love it with smoked salmon. But it is such an unusual food that I searched high and low for a recipe that could do justice to it. This is a dish that came to me by way of exploration. I was cooking for a colleague and wanted to serve caviar—but I wanted the caviar to be a surprise. I twirled a forkful of this pasta, dripping with cream, over a little mound of caviar in a bowl. It looked so plain and simple—until he dug in and found the caviar lurking beneath! This dish is also nicely made with trout or salmon roe.

A word on taste: I feel like a recipe that charts unfamiliar ground (in this case caviar) often doesn't instruct on the simplest thing: how is this dish supposed to taste? I wish you could provide aroma and taste on a page. The caviar is always salty, but the pasta needs to be seasoned in its own right. The pepper illuminates the salt of the caviar. The lemon zest is floral and adds lightness to the flavor; the lemon juice adds some needed acidity along with sour cream. The cream comes in to temper everything and make sure the dish rides the line between acidic and rich.

SERVES 4

To make the sauce:
1 cup heavy cream
1 cup sour cream
Kosher salt and black pepper
A few grates of zest and juice of ½ to 1 lemon

In a large skillet, whisk together the heavy cream and sour cream. Season with salt and pepper. Simmer the cream mixture over medium heat to reduce it, whisking until it thickens and all of the sour cream melts, 2 to 3 minutes. Add the lemon zest and some lemon juice. Taste for seasoning. At this point, the sauce should be thick enough to coat the pasta.

(continued)

To cook the pasta:
4 oz dried angel hair pasta
1½ to 2 oz American caviar or trout roe
1 small bunch chives, minced

In a large pot, bring 6 qt water to a rolling boil. Add 2 Tbsp salt and bring the water back up to a boil. Add the pasta to the pot and cook until al dente, stirring occasionally to make sure it doesn't clump or stick to the bottom as it cooks, for about 2 minutes. Drain the pasta in a colander, reserving ½ cup of the cooking liquid.
Add the pasta to the skillet and toss to coat with the cream. Shut the heat off and allow the pasta to rest in the sauce for 2 minutes, tossing to coat from time to time. If the sauce is too thin, simmer over low heat for 2 additional minutes. If it is too thick, simply thin it out with some of the reserved pasta water. Taste for seasoning. Add more salt or lemon if needed.

To serve the pasta: Spoon a small amount of caviar in the center of 4 serving bowls. Use a fork to twirl the pasta and make a large forkful. Use your index finger to gently coax the pasta off the fork and on top of the caviar in the plate. Ideally, the pasta should hide the caviar. Spoon any leftover sauce over the pasta. Repeat with the remaining plates.

Note: The sauce thickens quickly so keep it loose with a little pasta water, if needed, as you plate. Sprinkle with the chives, a touch more grated lemon zest and serve immediately.

CHEF ALEX GUARNASCHELLI, Food Network star and Chef of **Butter Restaurant**, began her culinary career after graduating from Barnard College and working under the tutelage of the acclaimed American chef and restaurateur, Larry Forgione. Forgione encouraged Guarnaschelli to travel and expand her skill set, so she moved to France to do a work study at La Varenne Culinary School in Burgundy. After school and traveling throughout France, she moved to Paris to begin a four day stint at the Michelin three-star restaurant **Guy Savoy**. Four days turned into four years with Guarnaschelli rapidly being promoted to sous chef at **La Butte Chaillot**, another Savoy establishment. After seven successful years in France, Guarnaschelli returned stateside. Though she left the country, she maintained her connection with the cuisine, joining the venerable Daniel Boulud at restaurant **Daniel**, where she quickly rose through the ranks to become sous chef at **the Manhattan standard**. Always looking to expand her culinary knowledge, Guarnaschelli moved to Los Angeles for two years to join Joachim Splichal's Patina Group, where she worked at the acclaimed **Patina** restaurant in West Hollywood before moving to New York to open Splichal's first New York City venture. In 2003, Guarnaschelli became the executive chef at Butter Restaurant, where she would create her own eclectic American and green market-inspired menu. In addition to her restaurant work, Guarnaschelli inspires budding chefs as a Chef-Instructor at New York City's Institute of Culinary Education. In 2015, Chef Guarnaschelli opened **Driftwood Room** at Nautilus South Beach in Miami, Florida.

Chef Guarnaschelli is a recurring judge on the popular prime-time series "Chopped" and was featured on her own shows, "The Cooking Loft" and "Alex's Day Off." She has appeared on the Food Network's "Iron Chef America" as both a challenger and a judge and competed on season 4 of "The Next Iron Chef." In 2012, she bested nine rival chefs to win "The Next Iron Chef: Redemption" and joined the ranks of Kitchen Stadium Iron Chefs. Alex is a mentor on the second season of Food Network's "All-Star Academy," which premiered in 2016. Alex released her debut cookbook *Old-School Comfort Food: The Way I Learned to Cook* in 2013. Chef Guarnaschelli has supported Alex's Lemonade Stand Foundation for a number of years including participating in their signature culinary events, donating her prizes from Food Network competitions and hosting Lemon: NYC.

Chorizo and Clams

DAVID LENTZ

Since 2005, Chef David Lentz and The Hungry Cat have offered the highest quality seafood and meats matched with Southern California's abundant seasonal produce. This dish focuses on the artisan, combining the freshest shellfish with flavors south of the border.

SERVES 4

To make the soffritto:

½ cup extra virgin olive oil
2 chili de árbol
1 sprig rosemary
1 cup diced white onion
¼ cup sliced garlic
½ cup chopped red peppers
1 cup sherry
1 Tbsp hot paprika
1 Tbsp smoked paprika
Kosher salt
Black pepper

In a heavy gauge pot, heat ¼ cup extra virgin olive oil, add the chili and rosemary. Cook for 1 minute and add the onions, garlic and peppers and sweat. Add the sherry and reduce until dry. Add the paprika, season to taste and add the remaining extra virgin olive oil. Cook on low heat for 15 minutes.

To make the braised Tuscan black kale:

2 bunches Tuscan black kale
6 Tbsp extra virgin olive oil
1 small sprig rosemary
1 chili de árbol
½ cup sliced onions
2 cloves garlic, thinly sliced
Kosher salt
Black pepper

Remove the rib from the kale; blanch the kale in salted boiling water. Remove and squeeze out all the water. In a heavy gauge pot, add ¼ cup extra virgin olive oil, chili and rosemary. Sweat, add sliced onion and garlic and cook until translucent. Add the kale, season with salt and pepper. Add the remaining 2 Tbsp extra virgin olive oil and braise kale on low heat until the kale absorbs the seasoned oil. Add oil as needed if the kale gets too dry and cook for about an hour until the kale is very soft.

(continued)

To make the chorizo and clams:

2 Tbsp extra virgin olive oil
1 ½ cups Mexican chorizo (soft)
Soffritto (recipe on page 33)
1 ½ cups cooked garbanzo beans
Braised Tuscan black kale (recipe on page 33)
60 manila clams
1 cup sherry
1 cup chicken stock
2 Tbsp butter
Juice of ½ a lemon
1 Tbsp chopped parsley
2 Tbsp aioli
4 thick slices of grilled bread
Kosher salt
Black pepper

Heat a heavy gauge sauce pan on medium heat. Pour in the olive oil, heat for 1 minute, add the chorizo and render until cooked. Add the soffritto, cook 3 minutes and then add the beans, kale and clams. Stir well and then deglaze with the sherry. Cover and cook about 3-4 minutes until the clams open and the sherry is reduced by 3/4. Pour in the chicken stock, add the butter and reduce the heat. Season with salt, pepper and the lemon juice. Taste for seasoning and sprinkle in the parsley. Serve in a bowl with a generous spoon of aioli on top and the grilled toast.

Born and raised on the Chesapeake, **CHEF DAVID LENTZ** is the founder and chef of California's premiere seafood restaurant, **The Hungry Cat** in Hollywood. David grew up swimming in the Atlantic's estuaries, watching the local watermen unload the catch of the day to the docks filled with awaiting restaurateurs. David cut his teeth on the East Coast's indigenous seafood: soft shell crab, blue crab, clams, scallops, oysters, striped bass, mackerel and flounder. Seafood being David's true calling, it didn't fully register to him until he Jack Kerouac-ed it through U.S. restaurants and culinary hotspots, going from sous chef at the **Delano** in Miami to opening chef of the **China Grill** in Las Vegas.

While cooking in these ashy kitchens, whispers of David's simple Chesapeake past, warm afternoons, family and friends, barefeet, picnic tables covered in newspaper, buckets of fresh crab spilled across them and cold beer, materialized in the basic ingredients of a simple piece of fresh fish, a ripe tomato, a fresh clam.

Rooted in his past, the vision of Lentz's future began to emerge upon moving to Los Angeles. Working as a line cook at the California farm-to-table inspired, **Campanile**, he was mentored by the world renowned Mark Peel and Nancy Silverton. There, he developed his signature artisanal style of building relationships with farmers and fishermen, creating a seasonal approach to food and best of all, nurturing his relationships with his restaurant cooks and staff.

Finally, with a culinary vision based on his Chesapeake Bay childhood food memories, his restaurant experience in excellence and his deep connected relationships with local farmers and fishermen, in 2004 David opened his restaurant The Hungry Cat. It was a huge success, with a cult-like obsession for David's innovative pairing and presenting of ingredients.

Now married to chef Suzanne Goin and the father of three children, David and Suzanne, were incredibly touched by the story of Alexandra Scott and her lemonade stand. Every summer, Goin and Lentz use their culinary muscle to gather chefs nationwide for their fundraising event L.A. Loves Alex's Lemonade. Since 2010, they have raised millions of dollars to fund childhood cancer research.

David Lentz can also be seen on Esquire Network's "Knife Fight." He has participated in food festivals like Crabfest and Oysterpalooza, competed in “Lobster Rumble” for Tasting Table and has been covered extensively in *The Los Angeles Times, L.A. Weekly* and *The New York Times* among other publications.

//////

Louisiana Creole Gumbo (Rouxless Gumbo)

DONALD LINK

New Orleans chef Donald Link was born and raised in the Cajun town of Lake Charles, Louisiana and this rustic gumbo, which is often served at his St. Charles Avenue restaurant Herbsaint, always reminds him of home. Featuring okra, chicken, shrimp and his homemade pork sausage, this recipe includes two types of peppers as well as Cajun spices. The result is a dark, thick, rustic stew with just the right amount of heat.

SERVES 6 TO 8

To make the stock:

4 Tbsp olive oil
3 stalks celery, rough chopped
1 small onion, rough chopped
1 tsp black peppercorns
4 bay leaves
3 garlic cloves
Shrimp shells and heads
5 sprigs thyme
4 qt chicken stock, low sodium

For the stock, in a large pot heat olive oil. Add all remaining stock ingredients except for the chicken stock. Sauté for 4 to 5 minutes. Add chicken stock and bring to a boil. Reduce heat and simmer for about 45 minutes. Strain stock, pressing all liquid out of the shells and reserve stock.

To make the gumbo:

1 large onion, diced to yield 3 cups
5 celery stalks, diced to yield 2 cups
2 poblano peppers, seeded and diced
3 jalapeños, seeded and diced
4 Tbsp dried shrimp, rough chopped
3 Tbsp olive oil
8 cups okra, sliced in ½" rounds
2 cups tomatoes, diced
6 garlic cloves, thinly sliced
1 tsp oregano, fresh dried, hand crushed
1 whole chicken, cut into 12 pieces, skin on
1 Tbsp Kosher salt
2 tsp Cajun Spice
1 tsp file powder (optional)
4 bay leaves

(continued)

2 Tbsp vegetable oil
1 lb smoked Cajun pork sausage, cut into ½" semi circles to yield 3 cups
3 lb shrimp, peeled – reserve shells and heads for stock

To make the chicken:
Coat chicken with salt and Cajun spice. In a large cast iron pot, heat vegetable oil on a medium-high heat and sear the chicken skin side down until brown, approximately 5 minutes. Turn chicken and brown on second side for an additional 5 minutes. Remove the chicken and reserve. To the chicken pot, add onion, celery, poblanos, jalapeños, and dried shrimp and sauté until they are lightly browned, approximately 10 minutes. Remove from heat.

To assemble the gumbo:
In a large 8 qt pot, heat 3 Tbsp olive oil. Add okra and sear on a medium-high heat, approximately 10 to 15 minutes. When okra begins to stick to the pot, add tomatoes and garlic. Add chicken, sausage and sautéed vegetables to the okra pot. Cover with the stock. Bring to a boil, turn down heat and simmer uncovered. Add oregano, file and cook for an hour and a half, skimming fat that rises throughout the process. Add shrimp and simmer for 30 minutes more.

Inspired by the Cajun and Southern cooking of his grandparents, Louisiana native **CHEF DONALD LINK** began his professional cooking career at 15-years-old. Recognized as one of New Orleans' preeminent chefs, Chef Link has peppered the streets of the Warehouse District of New Orleans with several restaurants over the course of the past 15 years. Link's flagship restaurant **Herbsaint** earned him a James Beard Foundation Award in 2007 for "Best Chef: South." The same year, **Cochon** was nominated for "Best New Restaurant." Link was also nominated by the James Beard Foundation for the prestigious award of "Outstanding Chef" for multiple years. **Pêche Seafood Grill** was awarded "Best New Restaurant" at the 2014 James Beard Foundation Awards. *Gourmet Magazine* listed Herbsaint as one of the top 50 restaurants in America and was inducted into the Nation's Restaurant News Hall of Fame. Cochon was listed in *The New York Times* as "one of the top 3 restaurants that count" and recently named one of the 20 most important restaurants in America by *Bon Appétit*. For his commitment to the industry, the Louisiana Restaurant Association honored Link by naming him "Restaurateur of the Year" in 2012.

The James Beard Foundation also honored Link's first cookbook *Real Cajun: Rustic Home Cooking from Donald Link's Louisiana*, a collection of family recipes that Link honed and perfected while honoring the authenticity of the Cajun people, with their top award for "Best American Cookbook." In 2014, Link celebrated the release of his second cookbook *Down South: Bourbon, Pork, Gulf Shrimp & Second Helpings of Everything*, which looks beyond New Orleans and Louisiana at dishes in nearby states.

In 2015, Chefs Link and Stephen Stryjewski created the Link Stryjewski Foundation to address the persistent cycle of violence and poverty, as well as the lack of quality education and job training opportunities available to young people in New Orleans. Chef Link has participated in several Alex's Lemonade Stand Foundation culinary events including L.A. Loves Alex's Lemonade and Lemon: Chicago.

Jay's Italian Hot Peppers and Egg Pizza

JAY SCOTT, ALEX'S DAD H

Liz and Jay Scott enjoy entertaining in their back yard, making pizzas in a wood-fired oven that Jay built with his sons. They regularly auction off pizza parties at ALSF events, and they appreciate doing something they love for the generous supporters who bid on them. This particular recipe was inspired by supporters Aldo Gaspari and Steve Owens, who make an Italian long hot peppers and sharp cheese pie.

MAKES ONE SMALL OR MEDIUM SIZED PIZZA

2 to 3 Tbsp olive oil
6 roasted, seeded and halved Italian long hot peppers
5 to 6 slices of Cooper sharp American cheese
1 egg
Pizza dough (store bought or homemade)

Roll out the dough to the shape and size you desire. Spread olive oil on the dough. Spread the Italian long hot peppers evenly on pie.

Place in oven until dough is almost done. Remove pie from oven and cover with a single layer of Cooper cheese slices. Leave the center of the pie with no cheese. Crack an egg in the center of pie and put back in the oven.

Watch the pie closely. The cheese browns fast and the egg cooks quickly.

Remove and eat.

Alex (age 5) and Jay Scott

JAY SCOTT is Alex's dad and Co-Executive Director of Alex's Lemonade Stand Foundation and also proud father to three sons, Patrick, Eddie and Joey. Alex was diagnosed with neuroblastoma, a childhood cancer, when she was just 1-year-old. In 2000, at 4-years-old, Alex announced that she wanted to hold a lemonade stand to raise money to help find a cure for other children with cancer. In her lifetime, Alex would go on to raise over $1 million before she passed away in 2004 at the age of 8. Jay works alongside his wife Liz and the amazing staff, board of directors, sponsors and supporters to continue the fight against childhood cancer, one cup at a time. Jay loves basketball, distance running, dogs, making wooden bowls and hanging out with his family.

Braised Beef Short Rib Tacos

ROCCO WHALEN

A note from Chef Whalen: We serve these fork tender beauties in Korean tacos with kimchi but you can garnish more traditionally as well with anything you have fresh from the market. Letting the meat rest in its liquid will keep it from drying out.

This is a great marinade to use for braising as the cooking method. I prefer to marinate 24 hours before cooking.

To make ribs:

1 lb of short ribs, cut lengthwise but on the bone
4 Tbsp cane sugar
2 Tbsp chopped apples
1 Tbsp fresh chopped garlic
1 Tbsp fresh chopped ginger
Star anise, cinnamon or 5 spice, if you enjoy that flavor profile

Combine all ingredients. Marinate ribs in mixture and refrigerate.

After 24 hours together, the ingredients are ready to be gently removed from the ribs by hand (please don't rinse).

Place 1 medium skillet on medium-heat.

After 5 minutes, add 1 Tbsp blended or vegetable oil.

Season both sides of rib with salt and pepper.

Begin to sear for 3 to 5 minutes on each side until crust forms. Add ribs to a Dutch oven or deep casserole dish and prepare to cover the ribs in the braising liquid.

To make the braising liquid:

3 cups sake (or substitute Chardonnay)
3 cups mirin (or substitute Riesling)
1 cup soy sauce
1 cup chopped scallions
1 cup diced onion

Combine the ingredients and pour them over the meat. Braise the ribs covered for 3 hours

(continued)

at 300 degrees. When they are tender, allow them to cool in the liquid.

To make the tacos:

1 package corn or flour tortillas
1 bunch sliced radishes
1 bunch chopped cilantro
1 jar kimchi
8 oz sour cream
1 bunch sliced scallions

Soften the tortillas over dry heat and keep warm by wrapping in a clean dish towel.

Slice your garnishes, i.e., radish, cilantro, scallions, avocado, etc. (this is where you can make them your own by adding any topping you like).

Remove the ribs from the liquid. The bone will slip right off. Bring the braising liquid to a boil and reduce until it's a glaze. Chop the meat and add to the glaze.

Build tacos!

CHEF ROCCO WHALEN opened his remarkable restaurant, **Fahrenheit** in historic Tremont, a stone's throw from downtown Cleveland in 2002. It is contemporary American cuisine, always in a state of flux and perfection. Rocco has emerged as one of the best chefs in Cleveland and in the Midwest. *Gourmet* magazine listed Fahrenheit in its "Guide to America's Best Restaurants." In 2004, he was a James Beard Foundation rising star nominee. *Esquire* magazine's food and travel writer, John Mariana, in his 2002 annual report of thc "Best New Restaurants in America," said "[Rocco] is a chef to keep your eye on." Additionally, Crain's *Cleveland Business* included Rocco in its 2013 annual report, "Forty under 40." Also in 2013, *Cleveland Magazine* named Rocco one of the city's most interesting people. In 2014, Rocco opened **Fahrenheit Charlotte** to rave reviews - the city's first open-air rooftop restaurant. Rocco also has starred in the Food Network show "The Fat Chef." Rocco has served his food at several Alex's Lemonade Stand Foundation culinary events including The Great Chefs Event in Philadelphia, Lemon: NYC and L.A. Loves Alex's Lemonade.

//////

Vegetable Parmesan

GIADA DE LAURENTIIS K

A note from Chef De Laurentiis: Adding marinara and cheese to vegetables is a fun way to mix up classic eggplant parmesan... and a great way to get kids to eat their veggies! It's a crowd pleaser for everyone.

SERVES 4 TO 6

Butter for greasing
Olive oil for drizzling
Kosher salt and freshly ground black pepper
1 medium eggplant, cut into ¼" to ½" thick slices
2 medium fennel bulbs, trimmed and sliced into ¼" thick pieces
1 red bell pepper, cut into thirds
1 yellow bell pepper, cut into thirds
1 orange bell pepper, cut into thirds
1 (26 oz) jar marinara sauce
3 cups shredded mozzarella cheese
1 cup grated Parmesan cheese
1 cup plain breadcrumbs

Place a grill pan over medium-high heat or preheat a gas or charcoal grill. Place an oven rack in the center of the oven. Preheat the oven to 375 degrees. Butter a 9" x 13" glass baking dish.

Drizzle the eggplant slices, fennel slices and peppers with olive oil. Season with salt and pepper. Grill the vegetables for 3 to 4 minutes each side until softened.

Spoon ¾ cup of the marinara sauce over the bottom of the prepared baking dish. Arrange the eggplant slices on top. Sprinkle with 1 cup of mozzarella cheese and ⅓cup of Parmesan cheese. Arrange the peppers in a single layer on top. Spoon ¾ cup of marinara sauce over the peppers. Sprinkle with 1 cup of mozzarella cheese and ⅓ cup of Parmesan cheese. Place the fennel on top and cover with the remaining sauce. Sprinkle the remaining cheeses on top. Sprinkle the breadcrumbs over the cheese and drizzle liberally with oil. Bake for 30 to 35 minutes until the top is golden and forms a crust.

Cool for 10 minutes before serving.

Cook's Note: The vegetables can also be baked in a 375-degree oven for 15 to 20 minutes until softened.

Printed with permission from the Food Network's "Giada at Home".

CHEF GIADA DE LAURENTIIS is the Emmy award-winning television personality of Food Network's "Everyday Italian" and "Giada at Home," a judge on Food Network Star, a NBC "Today" correspondent, successful restaurateur with her debut restaurant **GIADA** in Las Vegas, and author of eight *The New York Times* bestselling cookbooks, including her most recent, *Happy Cooking*, a collection of Giada's recipes and tips for leading a healthy and happy life, in addition to her latest children's book series, *Recipe for Adventure*.

Giada has been a fierce supporter in the fight against childhood cancer, being involved with Alex's Lemonade Stand Foundation since 2011 as an advisory board member for L.A. Loves Alex's Lemonade. Her annual involvement includes participating in L.A. Loves Alex's Lemonade, participating in an auctioned women chefs' dinner and a dinner at her restaurant, GIADA Vegas.

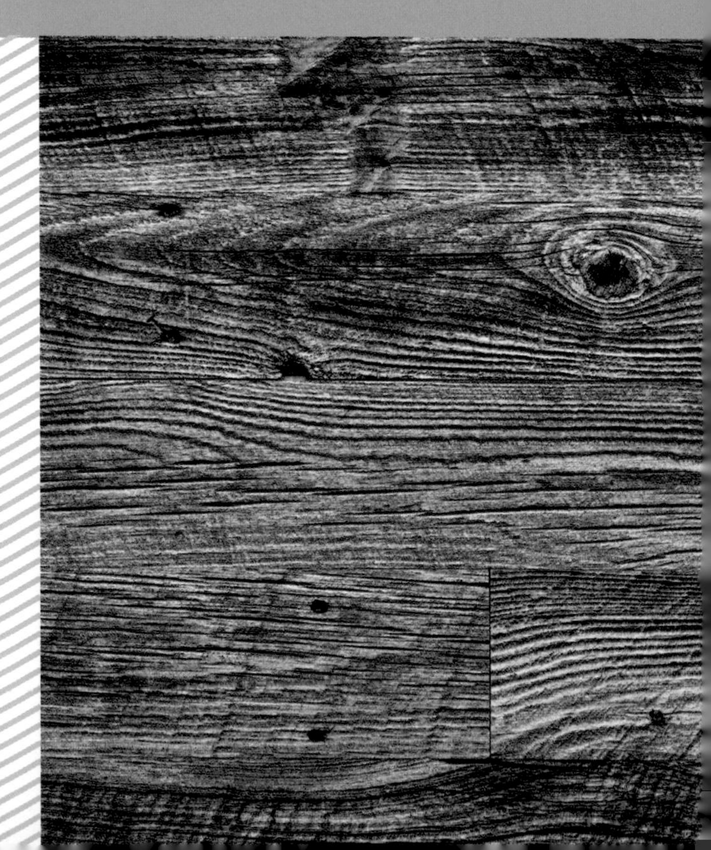

Giada

Grilled Fish Tacos with Radish Cucumber Slaw

MARY SUE MILLIKEN

Fish tacos originated in San Diego and Baja California. Although the classic Baja fish tacos are fried, this recipe grills them for a lighter taste that complements the avocado and grapefruit.

SERVES 4 TO 6

To make the grilled fish:

1 ½ lb sustainable fillet of fish
Extra virgin olive oil, for drizzling
Salt and freshly ground black pepper, to taste

Preheat a medium-hot grill, broiler oven or pan on the stovetop over medium-high heat. Drizzle the fish with olive oil, season with salt and pepper and cook until barely done, for 2 to 5 minutes per side, depending on the thickness. Remove the fish from the grill or pan, let cool slightly and then pull apart into large flakes.

To make the radish cucumber slaw:

4 pickling cucumbers, skin on, cut in half widthwise, fine julienne on mandoline
¼ small jicama, peeled, fine julienne
6 red radishes, fine julienne
2 habaneros, stemmed, seeded, fine julienne
¼ bunch cilantro, chopped
⅓ cup freshly squeezed lime juice
¾ cup extra virgin olive oil
2 tsp agave syrup
Sea salt and freshly ground black pepper, to taste

Place all the ingredients in a bowl, combine well and let stand, covered, for at least 30 minutes. You can store this salsa in the refrigerator up to 48 hours.

To assemble the tacos:

12 4" to 6" corn tortillas, warmed
Crema, crème fraiche or sour cream
Lime juice and zest
6 lettuce leaves, torn in half
Radish cucumber slaw
Avocado, peeled, seeded and sliced, for garnish
Pink grapefruit, peeled and segmented, for garnish

(continued)

In a bowl, mix crema, lime juice, zest and salt. Whisk until thoroughly combined.

To warm the tortillas, dip corn tortillas in water, shaking off excess. Toast, in batches, in a nonstick pan over moderate heat, about 1 minute per side. Wrap in towel to keep warm. Place the warm tortillas on a work surface.

Line each with a piece of lettuce and top with chunks of fish. Top each with a very generous spoonful of radish cucumber slaw with lots of juice. Drizzle lime crema mixture, finish with slice of avocado, one grapefruit segment and serve immediately.

CHEF MARY SUE MILLIKEN, a pioneer of world cuisine since the creation of **City Café** and **CITY** in Los Angeles in the 1980s, is most notably recognized as a preeminent ambassador of modern Mexican cuisine with her **Border Grill Restaurants and Trucks** (Los Angeles, LAX, Las Vegas). In 2014, she and longtime business partner, Susan Feniger, opened a second location in Las Vegas at The Forum Shops at Caesars.

Mary Sue has co-authored five cookbooks, co-starred in nearly 400 episodes of the Food Network's "Too Hot Tamales," and co-hosted a food-centered radio show for over a decade in Los Angeles. She competed on season three of Bravo's "Top Chef Masters," making it to the finale and winning $40,000 for her charity, Share Our Strength, and its mission to end childhood hunger in America. Chef Mary Sue has supported Alex's Lemonade Stand Foundation by participating in the L.A. Loves Alex's Lemonade, The Great Chefs Event and Lemon: NYC culinary events.

Grilled Ramen and Cheese

JONATHON SAWYER (K)

A note from Chef Sawyer: This is a really fun way to reinterpret ramen noodles. I like to think about these cuties almost like potato latkes, gently assembled and easy to pick up. At Noodlecat, we serve this with creamy tomato soup mixed with miso, but I also love it with onion dip or hummus.

SERVES 4

16 oz fresh ramen noodles
1 Tbsp salted butter
1 bunch scallions, sliced
1 clove garlic, smashed
1 tsp paprika
Salt and pepper, to taste
2 cups shredded aged cheddar cheese
½ cup grated Parmesan cheese

Fill a pot with water and season with salt until it tastes like seawater. Bring to a boil over high heat. Cook the ramen noodles for 8 minutes. Strain them but do not rinse them; you want that extra starch.

In the large bowl, combine the hot ramen noodles, butter, scallions, garlic, paprika, and salt and pepper. Allow the ramen to cool slightly, and then fold in the cheeses. You want to stir gently, but it's okay if the noodles tear a little.

Line a 9" x 13" baking dish with lightly greased parchment paper. Transfer the ramen mixture to the pan and spread evenly to form a ramen cake. The cake should be 1½ to 2½" thick. Top the mixture with another piece of lightly greased parchment paper. Place soup cans on top of the parchment paper to compress the cake. Refrigerate the ramen cake for at least 2 hours and up to 24 hours.

Once the ramen cake has cooled, turn it out onto a cutting board, still layered with the parchment. Cut the cake, still in the parchment paper, into 3" squares.

Remove the parchment paper and press each ramen cake in a panini press at medium heat until golden brown, about 10 minutes.

As a proud Clevelander, award-winning **CHEF JONATHON SAWYER** has worked tirelessly to help elevate the culinary landscape of his hometown with his distinctive restaurant concepts including **Trentina**, an intimate, fine-dining restaurant focusing on the cuisine of Trentino in Northern Italy, where his wife, Amelia Sawyer, and her family originate. Trentina adds yet another highlight to Chef Sawyer's growing list of acclaimed Cleveland culinary destinations, including his flagship, **The Greenhouse Tavern**, a French and seasonally inspired gastropub named by *Bon Appétit* as one of the "Best New Restaurants" in 2009; and **Noodlecat**, a mash-up noodle house focusing on local ingredients, sustainability and top-tier ramen, with locations at Public Square and the historical West Side Market. In addition to his stand-alone concepts, Chef Sawyer has also made an impact on the stadium foodservice scene with three restaurants launched in 2012: **Sawyer's Street Frites** and **Sausage & Peppers** at the Cleveland Browns' First Energy Stadium; and **SeeSaw Pretzel Shoppe** at the Quicken Loans Arena, home of the Cleveland Cavaliers.

Chef Sawyer's passion, skill and creativity have been rewarded greatly since he arrived on the culinary scene. In 2010, *Food & Wine* magazine named him a "Best New Chef" and he's been nominated for a James Beard Foundation Award for "Best Chef: Great Lakes" in 2013 and 2014. In 2015, Chef Sawyer won the James Beard Foundation Award for "Best Chef: Great Lakes." In addition, Chef Sawyer has made several national television appearances including Bizarre Foods America with Andrew Zimmern, "Iron Chef America," "Dinner Impossible," "Unique Eats" and "Best Thing I Ever Ate." Chef Sawyer has supported Alex's Lemonade Stand Foundation by participating as a chef in The Great Chefs Event and Lemon: Chicago.

Clara Madia Gianfrancisco's Ravioli

DONNIE MADIA GIANFRANCISCO K

A note from Donnie Madia: I chose this recipe because my Aunt Rita and my mother Clara were great bakers and cooks. They were incredibly hospitable, welcoming friends, family and sometimes strangers into our home for meals. They would always cater family functions, showers, weddings and birthdays. Everyone in attendance would always be overwhelmed by the homemade Italian cooking and always leave full and happy with Rita and Clara's hospitality and love!

My mother's ravioli dough recipe was something that I would experience on Saturday afternoons when she would roll out the dough by hand with a rolling pin before there was any machinery to do such. This was a painstaking task that would take hours. Every flat surface of our house would become a landing pad for individual ravioli pieces. My bed would be covered in a white sheet of wax paper, same with our dining room table and another table in the basement. Hundreds upon hundreds of raviolis would be positioned on these flat surfaces to dry and go into bags to be frozen and pulled out later for upcoming Sunday meals. The best part of the ravioli dough was the fresh cut-off pieces that would be made into homemade spaghetti and cooked for me a la minute that evening, served with a light tomato sauce.

SERVES 6

To make the dough:

2 ½ cups flour
1 egg
1 ¼ cups water

Start by adding 1 cup water to flour and egg mixture. Gradually add more water if needed to form the dough. Cut off a piece of dough to roll out for ravioli. Dough should be rolled out not too thin, in about an 18" square piece. Always keep the large piece of dough covered when not using, occasionally working the covered dough. Any excess pieces of dough cut from ravioli can be worked back into the large piece of dough.

To make the cheese filling:

5 to 6 lbs ricotta cheese (drain cheese in a strainer ahead of time)
6 eggs (if cheese mixture is too dry, add another egg)
Approx. ¼ cup fresh parsley, chopped
½ cup grated Italian Romano or parmesan cheese
Salt to taste

Mix all ingredients very well—no lumps.

Put approximately 1 rounded tsp of ricotta cheese mixture on dough about every 4". When placing the ricotta mixture on dough, be sure to leave enough dough closest to you to bring over ricotta cheese mixture. After overlapping dough, cut the dough lengthwise where dough overlapped ends. Be sure you overlapped at least ½" for forking. Cut ravioli into ravioli size, allowing about ½" around cheese mixture. Fork around 3 sides.

As you are working with dough, be sure to sprinkle flour, so the dough does not stick. Dip fork into flour when forking around edges.

Cook ravioli in boiling water—they are done when the raviolis rise to the top.

Among the city's most acclaimed restaurateurs, Chicago-born **DONALD J. MADIA** has mastered the art of collaboration to execute his singular unerring instincts for style, atmosphere and hospitality. His unique blend of visionary inspiration, attention to detail and sense of unlimited possibility informs all he touches— as evidenced in **Blackbird**, **avec**, **The Publican**, **The Violet Hour**, **Big Star**, **Publican Quality Meats** and **Nico Osteria**. His gift for connecting talented individuals and business acumen was recognized by the James Beard Foundation in 2015 when he was awarded "Outstanding Restaurateur."

Madia forged a partnership with Executive Chef Paul Kahan that would ultimately lead to some of Chicago's most ground-breaking and memorable dining establishments. **One Off Hospitality Group** formed in 2011, as a natural progression to the existing family of restaurants, and carries the same spirit of hospitality imbued from Madia's mother. As the term "One Off" implies, each project is unique and may be the group's last; which is why each project is handled with the utmost attention to detail and character.

Donnie Madia's elegance and attention to detail extend beyond the realm of business, and into his identity. His life essentials, as encapsulated by *GQ*, "revolve around style [...] and experiences, much like the ones he creates every evening for his diners." At his core, Madia is a family man — dividing his time between his extensive One Off family, his beautiful wife Estelle and their son Bronson.

A consummate family man, Madia carries on the tradition of warmth and hospitality learned from his mother, Clara and her twin sister Rita. Their deeply instilled sense of values imparted a dedication to charitable involvement, most notably his commitment to Alex's Lemonade Stand Foundation and his leadership in the Lemon: Chicago event.

Strozzapreti

JENN LOUIS

A note from Chef Louis: In most of Italy, these dumplings are called gnocchi verdi (gnocchi with greens) and ricotta or ravioli gnudi ("nude ravioli" or ravioli filling without pasta). In Florence, they are called strozzapreti, or "priest stranglers." The story goes that a gluttonous priest, who loved these dumplings, ate so many of them so fast that he strangled himself by swallowing them whole. True story or not, these are some of my favorite dumplings. Don't worry, eat slowly and chew them well, and you will be fine.

SERVES 6

¾ lb Lacinato kale or white chard, ribs removed
5 Tbsp fresh breadcrumbs
2 eggs
1 cup + 2 Tbsp whole milk ricotta, homemade or store bought
1 cup + 1 Tbsp finely grated Parmigiano-Reggiano, plus more for serving
Freshly grated nutmeg
Kosher salt and ground black pepper
All-purpose flour for dusting
2 to 3 Tbsp unsalted butter, melted

Prepare an ice bath by filling a large bowl with ice and cold water. Bring a large pot filled with generously salted water to a boil over medium-high heat. Add the kale and blanch until tender, about 3 minutes. Remove immediately from the pot with tongs and transfer to the ice bath. When cool, drain the greens in a colander. Place the greens in a kitchen towel and wring until mostly dry. Finely chop and set aside.

In the bowl of a food processor, process the breadcrumbs until finely ground. Add the kale, eggs, ricotta, Parmigiano-Reggiano and a few swipes of nutmeg and process until well combined. Season with salt and pepper. Scrape the ricotta mixture into a bowl.

Line two baking sheets with parchment paper and dust with flour. Scoop a heaping spoonful of ricotta mixture with one teaspoon, and push it onto a prepared baking sheet with the back of a second teaspoon. With your hands, gently roll the strozzapreti around in the flour to coat. Repeat with the remaining dough. Make sure that the strozzapreti don't touch or they will stick together.

(continued)

(To store, refrigerate on the baking sheets, uncovered, for up to 2 days. Do not freeze strozzapreti.)

Bring another large pot filled with generously salted water to a simmer over medium-high heat. Add the strozzapreti and simmer until they float to the surface, 1 to 3 minutes. Make sure to keep the cooking water at a simmer, as a rapid boil can break apart the strozzapreti. Remove immediately with a slotted spoon to a serving platter or individual bowls. Drizzle with the melted butter and top with grated Parmigiano-Reggiano. Serve right away.

Reprinted with permission from Pasta By Hand *by Jenn Louis.*

CHEF JENN LOUIS is a Portland, Oregon based chef and cookbook author. She has competed on Bravo's "Top Chef Masters", was named one of *Food & Wine*'s "Best New Chefs," and her simple, sophisticated cooking style, utilizing seasonal Pacific Northwest ingredients, has earned her two nominations for the James Beard Foundation Award of "Best Chef: Northwest." Her debut cookbook, *Pasta By Hand* published in 2015, was nominated for an IACP Award from the International Association of Culinary Professionals in the category of "Single Subject Cookbooks." Her second cookbook, *The Book of Greens,* publishes in 2017.

Chef Jenn Louis has participated in many Alex's Lemonade Stand Foundation's events including The Great Chefs Event in Philadelphia, L.A. Loves Alex's Lemonade and Lemon: NYC. She is active with the Foundation through donating cookbooks, cooking classes, meals and more and is a big supporter of the ALSF mission.

Grilled Skirt Steak with Watercress Salad

MARC MURPHY

A note from Chef Murphy: Skirt steak is a seriously underrated cut of beef, which means it's affordable for the home cook. I love how this great, flavorful cut stands up to marinades. At Landmarc, we grill it and serve it with chimichurri-dressed watercress with a little crumbled blue cheese, so each bite is a tiny flavor bomb: steak, watercress, dressing and the punch of the blue cheese.

SERVES 4

To make the skirt steak:

½ cup olive oil, plus more for oiling the grill
¼ cup fresh thyme leaves
2 garlic cloves, minced
2 tsp freshly ground black pepper, plus more as needed
2 lbs skirt steak
Kosher salt

To marinate the steak:

In a large bowl, combine the olive oil, thyme, garlic and pepper. Add the steak, toss to coat, cover and refrigerate for at least 1 hour or preferably overnight. You can also do this in a large resealable plastic bag.

To grill the steak:

Preheat a grill or heat a grill pan over moderately high heat until hot.

Lightly dip several paper towels in oil and carefully wipe the grill grate. Remove the steak from the marinade, scraping off any excess. Just before cooking, season the steaks liberally with salt and pepper. Place the steak on the grill and cook for 3 to 4 minutes per side for medium-rare and 1 to 2 minutes longer for medium. Transfer the meat to a cutting board, tent with foil, and let stand for 10 minutes before slicing.

To make the chimichurri vinaigrette:

¼ cup extra virgin olive oil
2 Tbsp fresh flat-leaf parsley, finely chopped
2 Tbsp fresh cilantro, finely chopped
1 small garlic clove, minced
½ small red onion, finely diced
1 tsp red pepper flakes
1 tsp kosher salt
½ tsp freshly ground black pepper
2 Tbsp sherry vinegar

(continued)

While the steak is resting, combine the olive oil, parsley, cilantro, garlic, onion, red pepper flakes, salt and black pepper in a medium bowl. Right before serving, add the vinegar and whisk to combine.

To make the watercress salad and assemble the dish:

3 bunches (about 12 cups) watercress
1 cup marinated roasted red peppers (cut into thin strips)
Kosher salt
Freshly ground black pepper
½ cup (2 oz) crumbled blue cheese

Right before serving, toss the watercress, roasted peppers and chimichurri vinaigrette in a large bowl. Season to taste with salt and black pepper and divide among four large serving bowls. Sprinkle with the blue cheese. Slice the steaks against the grain into bite-size pieces and arrange over the watercress salad.

Recipes from SEASON WITH AUTHORITY: Confident Home Cooking by Marc Murphy.

After attending the Institute of Culinary Education, **CHEF MARC MURPHY** apprenticed at restaurants in France and Italy before returning to New York where he landed a job as a line cook at Terrance Brennan's **Prix Fixe**. He stayed there for almost two years, working his way through every station in the kitchen and forging a professional bond with Brennan's sous chefs, Joseph Fortunato and David Pasternak. Murphy returned to Europe landing a position at the one-star **Le Miraville**, and then at the famed **Louis XV** in Monte Carlo and at **Le Cirque** once he returned to the states. Following Le Cirque, he worked as a sous chef at **Layla** and Executive Chef at **Cellar in the Sky** at Windows on the World. After receiving critical acclaim, including a two-star review from *The New York Times*, Murphy headed uptown to serve as Executive Chef of **La Fourchette** where the *Times'* critic Ruth Reichl awarded him another glowing two-star review.

In 2004, Murphy opened his first solo enterprise with **Landmarc** [Tribeca], which won rave reviews both for its eclectic French and Italian menu as well as its highly untraditional wine list. Following its success, Murphy opened **Ditch Plains** in the West Village in 2006 and another Landmarc restaurant in the iconic Time Warner Center in 2007. In 2013, Murphy opened **Kingside** at the Viceroy Central Park serving his interpretation of New American cuisine. And in 2015, Murphy opened **Grey Salt**, a Mediterranean-inspired restaurant in Tampa, Florida. Murphy's restaurants now fall under the **Benchmarc Restaurants by Marc Murphy** name, where he acts as Executive Chef and Owner.

Today, Murphy's involvement in the industry moves beyond the restaurants as well, with a regular role as a judge on The Food Network's highest rated hit, "Chopped" and "Chopped Junior" as well as appearances on "Chopped After Hours," "Iron Chef America," "Guy's Grocery Games," "Beat Bobby Flay," "Worst Cooks in America," "Unique Eats," "The Best Thing I Ever Ate," "The Best Thing I Ever Made," "The Rachael Ray Show" and NBC's "Today Show" among others. Marc's debut cookbook, *Season with Authority: Confident Home Cooking* was released in 2015. Chef Murphy has supported Alex's Lemonade Stand Foundation by participating in The Great Chefs Event in Philadelphia and Lemon: NYC.

Ricotta Cavatelli with Veal Cheeks, Escarole, Oven Dried Tomatoes and Pecorino

JOEY CAMPANARO

A note from Chef Campanaro: Being from Philly, I remember when Alex's Lemonade Stand was an actual lemonade stand. It received an enormous amount of attention, rightfully so, and has evolved to be one of the most important fundraisers of our time. Fighting to end pediatric cancer is not just noble, it is necessary for the future of the human race. Whenever and wherever I am, I will be ready, willing and able to join the fight.

I put this dish on the menu when The Harrison opened in 2001. I've been making it since then and it's my favorite dish to make. It's still as rich, delicious and meaningful as it was on the menu of the first joint where I was Executive Chef.

SERVES 4 TO 6

To make the Cavatelli:

2 cups fresh ricotta cheese
2 large eggs
1 cup all-purpose flour

In a mixer, whip cheese and eggs together until smooth. Slowly add the flour until the dough pulls together but remains a little sticky. The dough needs to rest for at least 25 minutes, wrapped in plastic wrap and placed in the refrigerator. After it has finished resting, roll the dough out with flour, cut into 1" strips and then feed through a Cavatelli cutter (available in specialty cooking stores). Spread out the pasta on floured sheet pan.

To make the braised veal cheeks:

2 lb veal cheeks
1 cup red wine
1 carrot
1 onion
1 cup canola oil
1 celery
2 Tbsp chopped garlic
1 bunch basil
1 bunch thyme
2 cup veal stock
1 can whole peeled tomatoes
Salt and pepper

(continued)

First season and brown the veal in canola oil. Then add vegetables and brown them as well. At this point, add the herbs, wine and stock. Bring to a simmer and then put in the oven, uncovered for 2 hours to slowly braise. Pull the meat out of the braise when it is almost falling apart. Strain the liquid, skim the fat and reduce by ⅓. Allow the meat to cool and then clean off the fat.

To make the oven dried tomatoes and assemble the dish:

1 head chopped and cleaned escarole (escarole is very dirty and must be thoroughly cleaned)
3 blanched, peeled and halved Roma tomatoes
1 tsp fresh chopped garlic
1 cup grated Pecorino (locatelli is preferred)
Extra virgin olive oil, to finish

Blanch the Roma tomatoes drop in plenty of salted boiling water until the skin breaks then shock (remove and put into ice water). Now the tomato is easily peeled. Slow dry them in a low oven for 2 hours.

Have boiling salted water ready.

In a skillet, add olive oil and garlic. Just before the garlic browns, add escarole, braised veal, oven dried tomatoes and 6 oz of the reduced braising jus. The sauce is almost ready. Drop the Cavatelli in the boiling water until they float to the top then strain them. Add them to the sauce. Toss the pasta with grated Pecorino, chiffonade (long, thin strips) of basil and a few drizzles of olive oil. Pasta dish can also be topped with a dollop of fresh ricotta just before serving.

With a culinary approach rooted in his Italian grandmother's kitchen and honed in a range of America's top restaurants, **CHEF JOEY CAMPANARO** brings a lifelong affinity for Mediterranean cuisine to every dish he creates. Learning from the brightest minds in the business, Campanaro has worked with chefs including Neil Murphy, Joachim Splichal, Jimmy Bradley and Jonathan Waxman. It was while Campanaro was working for Murphy at **Symphony Café** that he first met good friend and future business partner, Mike Price. Campanaro became Chef de Cuisine of Universal Studios' Executive Dining Room before returning to New York to open **The Harrison**. He then moved on to head the kitchen as Executive Chef of **Pace** and reopened his catering business, **Blackfoot Consulting**. Campanaro continues to cater and consult for esteemed clients such as Martha Stewart, Mike Piazza, NBC and Condé Nast. In 2006, Campanaro opened **The Little Owl** which has enjoyed a continued buzz as one of New York's most exciting restaurants, receiving wide acclaim including a two-star review from *The New York Times*. The Little Owl has since been joined by **Little Owl – The Venue**, a private event space and culinary showroom.

In 2007, Campanaro teamed up with Price to open **Market Table** in Manhattan's West Village. The duo then opened **The Clam**, a seafood-centric restaurant just blocks from Market Table and The Little Owl. Campanaro and Price's partnership has been featured in *Food & Wine, Condé Nast Traveler, The New York Times, New York Magazine, Time Out, Travel + Leisure*, NBC's "Today" and many more. Chef Campanaro has supported Alex's Lemonade Stand Foundation by participating in The Great Chefs Event in Philadelphia and Lemon: NYC, as well as going the extra mile to champion the cause.

Stuffed Blue Crabs Grande-Mére

JOHN BESH

A note from Chef Besh: After a crab boil, I like to use the leftover crabs for this simple recipe. Leave as much of the juices as you can in those shells, stuff them and bake them until uniformly golden brown and hot in the middle.

SERVES 6

2 cups "picked" blue crab meat
2 shallots, minced
1 green onion, chopped
1 clove garlic, sliced
½ cup mayonnaise
½ cup fresh breadcrumbs
1 sprig fresh tarragon, minced
1 tsp crushed red pepper flakes
2 dashes ground allspice
2 pinches Creole spices
Salt
6 blue crab top shells
¼ cup extra virgin olive oil
¼ cup grated Parmesan cheese
½ cup dried breadcrumbs

Preheat oven to 400 degrees. Mix together the picked crab meat, shallots, green onions, garlic, mayonnaise, fresh breadcrumbs, tarragon, red pepper flakes, allspice and Creole spices in a mixing bowl. Season to taste with salt. Divide the crabmeat stuffing between the individual crab top shells.

Mix together the olive oil, Parmesan cheese and dried breadcrumbs in a mixing bowl. Sprinkle the breadcrumbs over the stuffing in the crab shells. Arrange the crab shells on a baking sheet. Bake until golden, 12 to 16 minutes.

CHEF JOHN BESH is a chef and native son dedicated to the culinary riches of southern Louisiana. In his 12 restaurants, event space, entrepreneurial pursuits and public activities, he aims to preserve ingredients, techniques and heritage. Besh's talent and drive have earned him kudos throughout his career: *Food & Wine* named him one of the "Top 10 Best New Chefs in America." He won the coveted James Beard Foundation Award for "Best Chef: Southeast" in 2006 and was inducted into the Foundation's "Who's Who" in 2014. Besh's cookbooks, *My New Orleans* and *My Family Table*, were each recognized with an IACP Award. His third cookbook, *Cooking From The Heart*, was published in 2013 and his latest cookbook, *Besh Big Easy*, was released in 2015.

Chef Besh hosts two national public television cooking shows based on the books, "Chef John Besh's New Orleans," which began airing in 2011, and "Chef John Besh's Family Table," which debuted in 2013. The John Besh Foundation works to preserve New Orleans' culinary heritage via initiatives such as the Chefs Move! scholarship program and microloans for local farmers. Chef Besh has supported Alex's Lemonade Stand Foundation by participating in Lemon: Chicago, The Great Chefs Event in Philadelphia and L.A. Loves Alex's Lemonade as well as donating trips to New Orleans for auctions and championing the cause.

Balsamic Barbeque Baby Backs

JON SHOOK & VINNY DOTOLO

A note from Chef Shook: Wrapping ribs in foil steams them so they stay moist and makes them really tender because the steam helps break down the tough tissues in the meat. We finish them off under the broiler with a swipe of our balsamic barbecue sauce. You can also make them ahead of time and finish them on a kettle grill to get a little smoky edge.

A note from Chef Dotolo: I'm a fan of smoked ribs, but if you crave a rack and don't have hours and hours to smoke them, these are great. This recipe proves that you can cut corners and still get an end result that's fall-off-the-bone good.

SERVES 6 TO 8

To prepare the ribs:

2 racks of pork baby back ribs divided in half
Canola or grapeseed oil
4 fresh flat leaf parsley sprigs
4 fresh thyme sprigs
4 garlic cloves, smashed
Salt to taste

Preheat your oven to 500 degrees. Place each half rack of ribs on a 2' long sheet of foil, shiny side up. Rub each half rack with some oil and sprinkle with the salt, then divide the herbs and garlic among the packets. Wrap the foil around the ribs tightly and place them in a roasting pan. Roast the ribs for 30 minutes, then reduce the oven temperature to 250 degrees and cook until the ribs are fork tender, about 1½ hours longer. Remove from the oven and carefully open the foil so the ribs are cool enough to handle, 15 to 20 minutes. Turn off the oven.

To prepare the barbecue sauce:

1 cup ketchup
12 oz bottle lager-style beer (1½ cup)
½ cup balsamic vinegar
1 red onion, diced
1 garlic clove, very finely chopped
½ cup packed light brown sugar
3 Tbsp honey
1½ Tbsp grainy mustard
1 to 2 tsp Tabasco sauce (depending on how tangy you like your ribs)
1 tsp Worcestershire sauce

(continued)

While the ribs roast, make the barbecue sauce. Whisk all of the sauce ingredients together in a medium saucepan, add ¼ cup water, and bring to a boil over medium-high heat. Reduce the heat to medium-low, keeping the sauce at a simmer and cook until it is thick, at least for 1 hour (in the restaurant, sometimes it is cooked for up to 3 hours, partially covered, for an intensely deep flavor).

Turn the oven to broil. Liberally brush the meaty side of the ribs with half of the sauce and broil until caramelized, 2 to 3 minutes (if you don't have a built-in broiling element in your oven, then crank the oven heat to 500 degrees and roast the ribs until the sauce is hot and bubbling). Transfer to a platter and serve with the rest of the barbecue sauce on the side.

Reprinted with permission from Two Dudes, One Pan: Maximum Flavor From a Minimalist Kitchen *by Jon Shook & Vinny Dotolo.*

Los Angeles **CHEFS JON SHOOK AND VINNY DOTOLO** are the owners of **animal**, **Son of a Gun**, **Trois Mec**, **Petit Trois**, **Jon & Vinny's** and **Trois Familia**. They have been credited with innovating and changing the dining scene in Los Angeles through their critically acclaimed restaurants.

Shook and Dotolo have received numerous nominations and awards including *Food & Wine's* 2009 "Best New Chef," StarChefs' 2008 "Rising Star Chef" and eight James Beard Foundation nominations including 2009's "Best New Restaurant" for animal, 2011's "Best Chef: Pacific," 2015's "Best New Restaurant" for Petit Trois, 2016's "Outstanding Restaurant Design" for Jon & Vinny's, and "Best Chef: West" in 2013, 2014, 2015 and won in 2016. In 2013, Shook and Dotolo formed a culinary partnership with Lexus and were named Culinary Masters. In 2015, Shook and Dotolo became the newest All-Clad Chef Ambassadors. A dream come true for Shook and Dotolo, they partnered with Vans and released a Chef Shoe Line collaboration for animal, Son of a Gun and Jon & Vinny's in 2016. Shook & Dotolo are supporters of Alex's Lemonade Stand Foundation by participating in The Great Chefs Event, Lemon: Chicago and L.A. Loves Alex's Lemonade.

Ziti with 'Nduja and Shrimp

TONY MANTUANO

A note from Chef Mantuano: I have been involved with ALSF for many years and it is a cause I truly believe in. I've participated in ALSF events all over the country and am passionate about raising awareness here in Chicago. I have so much respect for Alex's parents and all that they do, and it's so important to continue Alex's legacy.

I love to call this dish Calabrian surf and turf. 'Nduja is a spicy, spreadable salami that pairs surprisingly well with shrimp and pasta. The best 'nduja has a balanced sweet and hot pepper flavor that gives this dish another dimension.

SERVES 4

12 medium shrimp, peeled and cleaned
3 Tbsp extra virgin olive oil
Sea salt and freshly ground black pepper
2 oz 'nduja
1 lb ziti pasta
2 Tbsp chopped parsley

Bring a large pot of salted water to a boil. In a large skillet, heat the olive oil over medium-high heat. Add the shrimp. Season with salt and pepper. Cook for 2 minutes, turn the shrimp over and cook for 1 minute more. Add the 'nduja and break up with a wooden spoon to combine. Take off the heat and set aside until ready to use.

Meanwhile, add the pasta to the boiling water and cook until al dente, about 3 minutes less than what the box advises. Drain the pasta, reserving 1 cup of the pasta water. Return the pasta to the pot. Add the shrimp 'nduja mixture and the pasta water into the pot and cook over low heat, gently tossing the pasta with the sauce for 2 minutes to allow it to marry with the sauce and absorb it. The pasta should still be firm to the bite.

Transfer to a warmed platter.

Top with parsley and serve immediately.

James Beard Foundation Award winner, **CHEF TONY MANTUANO** is an influential culinary force, a chef who has been on the ground floor of defining true Italian cuisine in the United States. In addition to his role as chef partner at **Spiaggia**, Mantuano is the chef partner at **River Roast**, situated on the Chicago River; **Bar Toma**, an Italian neighborhood pizzeria and bar; **Terzo Piano**, a Mediterranean-inspired restaurant at The Modern Wing of the Art Institute of Chicago; and the owner of **Mangia Trattoria**, a classic Italian restaurant in his hometown of Kenosha, Wisconsin. Mantuano is a recipient of the James Beard Foundation Award for "Best Chef: Midwest" and *The Chicago Tribune's* "Good Eating Award." Outside of the kitchen, Mantuano is often recognized for his participation on season two of Bravo's "Top Chef Masters." Other projects include cookbook collaborations with Cathy Mantuano, a wine expert and former manager of Spiaggia. The husband and wife team authored *The Spiaggia Cookbook* and *Wine Bar Food*. Chef Mantuano helped create and co-host the Lemon: Chicago culinary event.

Beer Can Chicken

ADAM PERRY LANG

A note from Chef Lang: Propping a whole chicken on an open can of beer and slow-roasting it on the grill may seem a bit wacky, but the result is incredible. The beer vapors do little to moisten the chicken; rather, the vertical position of the bird allows its juices to flow down over the breast, keeping it succulent.

SERVES 4

To make garlicky barbecue marinade:

10 garlic cloves, coarsely chopped
¼ cup Worcestershire sauce
2 Tbsp low-sodium soy sauce
1 medium onion, chopped
¼ cup water

In a blender, puree the chopped garlic, Worcestershire sauce, soy sauce, onion and water. (The marinade can be refrigerated for up to 1 week).

To make seven-spice dry rub:

½ cup dark brown sugar
½ cup sweet paprika
¼ cup kosher salt
¼ cup chili powder
¼ cup dry mustard
1 tsp freshly ground black pepper
2 tsp Old Bay Seasoning
½ tsp ground ginger

In a small bowl, whisk together all of the ingredients.

(The dry rub can be refrigerated or frozen for up to 6 months).

To make cider mop spray:

1 cup apple juice
1 cup water
¼ cup cider vinegar

In a large, glass measuring cup, combine the apple juice, water and vinegar. Pour into a spray bottle and refrigerate.

(The mop spray can be refrigerated for up to 1 week).

To make sweet and sticky barbecue sauce mixed with ½ cup water:

½ cup vegetable oil
5 garlic cloves, chopped
1 medium onion, chopped
1 green bell pepper, chopped
Salt
¼ cup dark rum
3 Tbsp chili powder
1 Tbsp freshly ground black pepper
½ tsp ground allspice
½ tsp ground clove
1 cup dark brown sugar
2 cups water
2 cups ketchup
½ cup molasses
½ cup yellow mustard
½ cup cider vinegar
2 tsp hot sauce

Heat the oil in a large saucepan. Add the garlic, onion, green pepper and a large pinch of salt and cook over moderate heat, stirring occasionally, until softened, about 10 minutes.

Add the rum and simmer for 2 minutes. Add the chili powder, black pepper, allspice and cloves and cook, stirring, until fragrant, about 3 minutes. Add the brown sugar, water, ketchup, molasses, mustard, vinegar and hot sauce and simmer over moderate heat, stirring often, until thickened, about 30 minutes. Transfer the barbecue sauce to a large food processor and puree. Season the sauce with salt.

(The barbecue sauce can be refrigerated for up to 2 weeks).

(continued)

To make the chicken:
1 4 lb chicken
1 12 oz can of beer
1 cup hickory or other hardwood chips, soaked in water

Rub the garlicky barbecue marinade all over the chicken and refrigerate overnight or for 4 hours at room temperature.

Bring the chicken to room temperature and sprinkle the seven-spice dry rub all over the skin.

Light a charcoal fire in a covered grill and set it up for indirect grilling: when the temperature reaches 225 degrees, carefully push the hot coals to one side and place a drip pan filled with 1 cup of water on the opposite side. Alternatively, bring a smoker to 225 degrees. Discard (or drink) half of the beer. Stand the chicken upright on the can, with its legs pointing down.

Transfer the chicken on the beer can to the grill, setting it over the drip pan and cover the grill; you'll need to cook the chicken for about 3 hours total. To maintain the temperature at 225 degrees, replenish the charcoal with a fresh batch of burning coals every hour. Add more water to the drip pan when half of it is evaporated. After the first 45 minutes, rotate the chicken, then drain ½ cup of the wood chips and scatter them over the coals. After another 45 minutes, drain and scatter the remaining wood chips over the coals. Rotate the chicken again and spray the chicken with the cider mop spray. Rotate and spray the bird twice more, at 45-minute intervals. The chicken is done when an instant-read thermometer inserted in an inner thigh registers 165 degrees. Remove and discard the beer can. Transfer the bird to a carving board; let rest for 20 minutes.

Remove the drip pan from the grill. Stoke the coals and spread them in an even layer. Replenish with fresh coals to make a medium-hot fire. Cut the chicken in half through the backbone and brush it all over with the diluted Sweet and Sticky Barbecue Sauce. Grill the chicken, skin side down, until lightly charred. Turn and brush it with more sauce. Continue grilling, brushing and turning until the chicken skin is crisp and glazed, about 15 minutes. Serve at once.

Reprinted with permission from adamperrylang.com

Baby back ribs and pulled pork are just a taste of **CHEF ADAM PERRY LANG'S** repertoire, though. Adam's experience and expertise extends to barbecue and grilling in both the professional and home kitchens. After graduating with distinction from the Culinary Institute of America and working his way through the kitchens of top-rated French restaurants including **Le Cirque** and **Daniel** in New York City; and Restaurant **Guy Savoy** in France, Adam left his pursuit of reviewers' stars to follow his passion for barbecue.

Adam Perry Lang's first restaurant, **Daisy May's BBQ USA** is a classic rib shack in the heart of New York City. Famous for its whole pig, pulled pork and beef ribs, Daisy May's has been the 'go to joint' for barbecue lovers since it opened in 2003. **Barbecoa** is Adam's first global venture and is located in the center of London. Partnering with renowned chef Jamie Oliver, Barbecoa showcases live fire cooking methods from around the world. Adam has also partnered up with Mario Batali's Las Vegas steakhouse, **CarneVino**, as he sources and oversees the dry aging of the superior beef the restaurant is famous for.

Desiring to make barbecue and grilling as accessible for the home cook as he had for the customers in his restaurant, Adam's first book, *Serious Barbecue: Smoke, Char, Baste and Brush Your Way to Great Outdoor Cooking*, was a *The New York Times* best-seller. Adam was also featured on The Food Network's "Iron Chef America" and "What's Hot, What's Cool" and "BBQ with Bobby Flay" as well as several national news outlets. Adam's second book *BBQ 25*: *The World's Most Flavorful Recipes-Now Made Fool-Proof* has been breakthrough in simplifying 10% of the recipes you go to 90% of the time. Adam's book *Charred & Scruffed* offers bold new techniques for explosive flavor on and off the grill. Chef Lang has supported Alex's Lemonade Stand Foundation by participating in L.A. Loves Alex's Lemonade and The Great Chefs Event.

Three Meat Pasta H K

ASHER JAMES LEONARD

A note from Shannon, Asher's mom: As we all discussed Asher's favorites (or "best" as he always said, he never said something was his favorite or that he really liked it, he simply called it "my best") this dish stood out.

From the time he was very young, Asher always wanted to be in the kitchen cooking and baking, and he spent time playing "cooking" too. Even during times he was in the hospital for treatment, he would want to order food from the kitchen that he could "cook." He'd want the tacos so he could put them together himself, or he'd ask us to order him 5 different fruits so that we could chop it all up and make fruit salad. We have many wonderful memories of cooking, baking and eating with our sweet boy.

1 lb angel hair pasta
2 cups cooked chicken, diced
2 cups cooked sausage, crumbled
2 cups cooked ham, cubed
1 large yellow onion, chopped
2 cups cheddar cheese, shredded
16 oz cottage cheese
3 chicken bouillon cubes (or equivalent of chicken bouillon base)
1 cup hot water
1 Parmesan cheese, grated

Preheat oven to 350 degrees.

In a large pot, boil water for angel hair pasta. When cooked, drain and set aside.
In a large bowl, mix together the chicken, sausage, ham, onions, cheddar cheese and cottage cheese. Add pasta and mix to combine.

In a separate small pot, dissolve bouillon cubes in water. Pour over pasta mixture and mix well. If the mixture seems dry, add another ½ to 1 cup of water and corresponding bouillon.

Pour mixture into a 9" x 13" greased baking dish and top with the Parmesan cheese. Bake for 30 to 35 minutes or until the bubbling around the edges.

Freezes well; freeze unbaked.

ASHER JAMES LEONARD was the funniest, smartest, sassiest, most compassionate boy his family and friends had ever met. He had a smile on his face, a zest for life and an amazing ability to constantly put others before himself.

Though Asher was the little brother in a family with three boys, he always kept up with his big brothers, Caleb and Xavier, and did whatever they did. His older brothers taught him everything they knew about Star Wars and it wasn't long until he knew more than they did. He also loved football, LEGOs, playing video games with his brothers, Transformers, cooking and The Black Keys, his favorite band, whom he and his family had the pleasure of seeing in concert twice and meeting in person in 2013.

When Asher was two and a half, he complained that his neck hurt. Since he liked to roughhouse and play tackle football with his older brothers, his parents didn't think much of it. They were sure it was just a minor bump or bruise. When the pain continued for a few months, they took Asher to see the pediatrician. She completed a neurological workup, ordered a set of x-rays and found nothing that led her to believe something was "wrong." Asher's parents decided to give it a few more weeks, contemplated starting him in physical therapy and waited to see if the pain would get better. Asher continued to complain of neck pain, would no longer sit on his mother's lap to read a story and complained about being strapped into his car seat. On Friday, October 14, 2011, Asher had an MRI that revealed the cause of his neck pain. A large posterior fossa tumor was extending down his spinal column and causing his spinal cord to be compressed. In the blink of an eye, the healthy, happy, energetic baby boy was diagnosed with anaplastic ependymoma, a form of brain cancer.

Asher endured two lengthy brain surgeries, over a year's worth of different oral and IV chemotherapy regimens, six weeks of radiation, cyberknife radiation to two brain tumors and two more courses of radiation to problem tumors in his brain and spine.

Asher taught those who knew him how to appreciate life, smile, love and live every day as if it were the last. He never asked why he had to go through so much and he never got angry or frustrated at his situation, when there were many times he should have. His body took a beating from the cancer and treatments, he continued to live and appreciate what he could do, not dwell on what he was no longer able to do. In the last six months of his life, he was no longer able to walk, he wasn't always able to use his hands and arms, but he always had a smile on his face and the desire to keep on playing, talking, laughing, telling stories and interacting with his friends and family. Though Asher's spirit remained positive and strong, his body could take no more and he passed away on June 30, 2013.

His family continues to hope that their journey with Asher and his cancer battle will continue to bring awareness and inspire action against childhood cancer. As Team Asher's Storm Troopers, they have participated in numerous Foundation events to raise awareness and funds for childhood cancer research. His family knows that continued awareness is what will cause people to stop, listen and ultimately take action.

"WE KNOW THAT AWARENESS BRINGS FUNDING, FUNDING BRINGS RESEARCH AND RESEARCH WILL BRING THE CURE."

SIDE DISHES & STARTERS

Roasted Cauliflower with Curry and Red Wine Vinegar

SUZANNE GOIN

This curry-roasted cauliflower dish started as a staple "staff meal" at Chef Goin's restaurant but became so popular with the team that she decided to add it to the menu along with her other creative farmers market-driven recipes. The cauliflower becomes spicy, vinegary and caramelized but still crunchy. It's a side dish but can be served over rice or another grain to become a filling dinner.

SERVES 4 TO 6

¼ tsp coriander seeds
¼ tsp cumin seeds
1 tsp curry powder
1 ½ tsp bittersweet paprika
1 medium head cauliflower, cored and cut into florets
1 small yellow onion, peeled, cored and cut into sixths
2 Tbsp extra virgin olive oil
2 Tbsp unsalted butter, melted
1 ½ Tbsp red wine vinegar
1 Tbsp chopped cilantro
Kosher salt
Freshly ground black pepper

Preheat the oven to 450 degrees. Toast the coriander seeds in a small pan for a few minutes, until the seeds release their aroma and are lightly browned. Using a mortar and pestle, pound them coarsely. Repeat with the cumin seeds.

Combine the coriander, cumin, curry, paprika, 1 tsp salt and a few grindings of black pepper in a small bowl. Stir together to combine.

Place the cauliflower and onion in a large mixing bowl and pour the olive oil and melted butter over the top. Sprinkle the spice mixture over the cauliflower and toss well to coat the vegetables completely in the oil, butter and spices. Add the vinegar and toss again to combine well.

Place the cauliflower in a single layer on a baking sheet. Roast for about 30 minutes, stirring every 8 minutes or so until the cauliflower is tender and nicely caramelized. Scatter the cilantro over the cauliflower, toss with a large spoon and taste for seasoning.

In 1998, **SUZANNE GOIN** opened **Lucques** in West Hollywood with her business partner Caroline Styne. The restaurant met with instant success and Suzanne was named one of *Food & Wine*'s "Best New Chefs" in 1999. A second restaurant, **a.o.c.**, the groundbreaking concept of inspired wines by the glass with a small plates menu, opened in 2002 and was met with enthusiasm from the public and the press. Suzanne received two coveted awards from the prestigious James Beard Foundation in 2006 including "Best Chef: California." Her first cookbook, *Sunday Suppers at Lucques*, won "Best Cookbook from a Professional Viewpoint." Suzanne and Caroline ventured to the Westside of Los Angeles when they opened their largest and most glamorous restaurant, **Tavern**. Inspired by the success of their more casual Larder section of Tavern, Suzanne and Caroline opened **The Larder at Maple Drive** in 2011, followed by **The Larder at Burton Way** in 2013. Suzanne's second book, *The A.O.C. Cookbook* debuted in 2013 to glowing reviews in both the United States and Canada.

Suzanne and Caroline are among the most respected restaurateurs in California and continue to receive recognition for their food, beverage programs and service from *The Los Angeles Times, The New York Times, Wall Street Journal, L.A. Weekly, Condé Nast Traveler, Gourmet, Food & Wine, Bon Appétit, Saveur, Los Angeles Magazine, Angeleno, Zagat* and *Gayot.com*.

In 2011, she became a member of the International Culinary Panel of distinguished chefs for Singapore Airlines, developing her recipes for in-flight dining. Over the past few years, Suzanne and Caroline have been honored to prepare several fundraising dinners for both President Obama and First Lady Michelle Obama. Passionate about healthy sustainable food for children, Suzanne worked to create a partner school lunch program to Alice Waters' Edible Schoolyard project. Chef Goin is a co-founder and co-host, along with Chef David Lentz and business partner Caroline Styne, of L.A. Loves Alex's Lemonade, which has raised over $4 million for childhood cancer research since its inception in 2010. Finally in 2016, after multiple nominations, Suzanne won the coveted James Beard Foundation Award for "Outstanding Chef of the Year."

Taco Soup K

ALEX GORDON

This simple recipe is a great warming dish on a chilly day. With cans of veggies and packaged seasoning, it can be made quickly for an easy weeknight meal for the family to enjoy.

SERVES 4

1 lb hamburger meat
1 packet ranch dressing
1 packet taco seasoning
1 15 oz can of tomato sauce
1 can Rotel chilies, your choice
2 to 3 cans of chili beans, drained
1 to 2 cans of corn
Cheese, sour cream, tortilla chips and other toppings of your choice

Brown hamburger meat in a frying pan and drain the excess liquids. Mix in the ranch dressing and taco seasonings and cook for 1 to 2 minutes.

Pour in tomato sauce, Rotel with juices, drained chili beans and corn with juices. Cook on medium to medium-low for 20 minutes.

Top with cheese, sour cream and crushed tortilla chips and serve.

ALEX GORDON is a 2015 World Series Champion, Kansas City Royals All-Star left fielder and 4-time "Rawlings Gold Glove Award" winner. Drafted following his junior season at the University of Nebraska where he swept the collegiate baseball awards for "College Player of the Year," the "Golden Spikes Award," the "Dick Howser Award," the "Brooks Wallace Award" and the "ABCA Rawlings Player of the Year." In 2005, he was named the No. 1 college draft prospect by *Baseball America* as well as the second-best overall prospect, being drafted by the Kansas City Royals. A member of 2004 U.S. National Team, he helped Team USA to an 18-7 overall record, seeing a majority of his playing time at first base. In 2007, he began playing in the majors with the Royals and in 2011 transitioned to the outfield. In addition to his 2015 World Series Championship and Gold Glove awards, he has three "Fielding Bible Awards," a "Platinum Glove Award" and one "Wilson Defensive Player of the Year" distinction.

In 2014, Alex won the "Hutch Award," given each year to a Major League player who best exemplifies the honor, courage and dedication of baseball great Fred Hutchinson, both in on-field achievements and off-the-field work. Alex Gordon resides in Lincoln, Nebraska, with his wife, Jamie and their two sons. Alex has supported Alex's Lemonade Stand Foundation since 2006 as a local spokesperson and has hosted the Alex Gordon Classic since 2015, benefitting ALSF. In 2015, Gordon was honored as ALSF's "2016 Volunteer of the Year."

Watermelon and Feta Salad

MICHAEL SOLOMONOV

A note from Chef Solomonov: This combination seems straight out of modernist cuisine, but it's actually an old-school Bulgarian favorite. To me, it feels like summertime in Tel Aviv: a baby watermelon (seedless watermelons were invented in Israel!), cut into wedges, a slab of Bulgarit (Bulgarian feta) and oil-cured black olives. Once you taste it, you understand why the combination is such a classic: the briny and funky cheese is perfectly balanced with the sweet, juicy watermelon. I like to jazz it up with a bit of grassy za'atar, but this is a New World application; the Bulgarians never would have touched the stuff. This formula loves improvisation. Any kind of persimmon or another ripe melon would be great as a substitute for the watermelon. In the fall, I like to use fragrant figs. The cheese is interchangeable too. French chefs serve watermelon with goat cheese. In Bulgaria, where the feta is often made from cow's milk, they will sometimes substitute an aged sheep's milk kashkaval cheese for a nuttier effect.

SERVES 4

½ small watermelon, rind removed and cut into 1" wedges (4 cups)
Kosher salt
⅓ cup pitted oil-cured black olives
¼ cup olive oil, plus more for drizzling
½ cup crumbled feta
¼ cup toasted pistachios, chopped
2 Tbsp chopped fresh mint

Arrange the watermelon on a platter and season well with salt.

Combine the olives and oil in a food processor and puree until smooth. Spoon the puree on the watermelon, then the feta, pistachios and mint. Drizzle on a bit more oil.

Reprinted with permission from ZAHAV: A World of Israeli Cooking *by Michael Solomonov and Steven Cook.*

A 2011 James Beard Foundation Award winner for "Best Chef: Mid-Atlantic" and a 2016 James Beard Foundation Award winner for "Best International Cookbook" and "Book of the Year" for his and business partner/co-author Steven Cook's first cookbook, *Zahav: A World of Israeli Cooking*, **CHEF MICHAEL SOLOMONOV** is the Executive Chef at **Zahav**, Philadelphia's renowned modern Israeli restaurant. In addition to his duties at Zahav, which he co-owns, Chef Solomonov is a partner in **Federal Donuts**, a mostly take-out, donuts-and-fried-chicken shop serving exceptional coffee, cake, donuts and fried chicken. He is also a partner in **Abe Fisher**, which focuses on adventurous takes on old-world Jewish cuisine, as well as **Dizengoff**, an authentic, Israeli-style hummusiya. In 2016, Chef Solomonov was a finalist for "Outstanding Chef" at the James Beard Foundation Awards, and Abe Fisher was a semifinalist for "Best New Restaurant" in 2015. Chef Solomonov was also voted *Eater's* "Chef of the Year" and was featured in *Esquire's* September 2014 issue as one of "22 Men Redefining Style Across America." Chef Solomonov has participated in Lemon: Chicago and annually in The Great Chefs Event in Philadelphia as a chef and has donated dinner as an auction item. He adds, "Alex's Lemonade Stand Foundation has a particularly huge impact because when you raise money for research, there's something very tangible about the results. Particularly now that I have two young children of my own, it just becomes more real."

Insalata Zucca K

JONATHAN WAXMAN

This summery, light dish is a refreshing complement to any summer meal. The touch of Parmesan cheese will bring out the flavor and aroma of the salad.

SERVES 4

3 medium summer squash
1 cup crushed marcona almonds
Extra virgin olive oil
1 piece of Parmesan cheese
1 lemon, juiced
Salt & pepper to taste

Lightly toast almonds in a dry pan over medium-low heat for 3 minutes. Immediately season with a pinch of salt. Set aside and cool.

Shave summer squash lengthwise on a mandoline 1⁄16" thick. The squash should be thin enough to easily fold but thick enough to hold its shape.

Lay almonds between two pieces of parchment paper and gently crush with a heavy rolling pin or pan.

Place squash in a mixing bowl. Season with salt, pepper, lemon juice and extra virgin olive oil. Gently toss to keep the squash intact.

Gently fold in crushed almonds and grated Parmesan and serve.

Working as a successful chef, restaurateur and author,

CHEF JONATHAN WAXMAN has graced such prestigious kitchens as **Chez Panisse** in Berkeley and **Michael's** in Los Angeles. Waxman went on to open his own restaurant in New York City — **Jams**, described by *The New York Times* as "a culinary comet," as well as the famed Washington Park. Today, Waxman is the chef and owner of **Barbuto** in Manhattan's West Village. His first cookbook, *A Great American Cook*, was published in 2007 and his second book, *Italian My Way*, was released in 2011.

He participated in two seasons of "Top Chef Masters" on Bravo, where he earned the nickname "Obi-Wan Kenobi" and Jonathan Gold of *The Los Angeles Times* has referred to Jonathan as "the Eric Clapton of chefs." Giving back is important to Waxman and he works closely with many charities including City Meals on Wheels. Chef Waxman has supported Alex's Lemonade Stand Foundation by founding Lemon: NYC, and participating in The Great Chefs Event and L.A. Loves Alex's Lemonade culinary events.

Charcoal Potatoes

MICHAEL VOLTAGGIO

Inspired by a dish Michael Voltaggio learned from mentor and chef José Andrés called Papas Islas Carnarius, a wrinkled potato dish that originated in the Canary Islands. This recipe takes the basic combination of potatoes, sour cream and chives and transforms them into a modern creative dish by cooking in salty water stained with squid ink. The result looks like lumps of coal, with salt crystals on the skin and a tasty, soft interior and served with house-made sour cream.

SERVES 2 TO 3

To make the sour cream:

1 qt cream
½ cup buttermilk

Make one week in advance.

Whisk the cream and the buttermilk thoroughly and transfer into clean airtight container (i.e mason jar, Tupperware).

Leave out at room temperature for 3 days then move to refrigerator for at least 2 days before use.

To make the potatoes:

4 Tbsp kosher salt
3 Tbsp squid ink
4 cups water
12 golf ball sized potatoes (red potatoes, Yukon gold, purple potatoes, etc.)
Chopped chives, Chinese black vinegar, white vinegar powder, to taste

Wash potatoes and place in a single layer in the bottom of a 6 qt stockpot. Mix salt and squid ink plus water in a bowl and whisk together.

Pour mixture water over potatoes, just enough to cover. Bring to a boil and leave boiling until all the liquid is reduced to a small layer in bottom of the pot. Shake stockpot vigorously back and forth to coat the outside of the potatoes with the dry mixture. Potatoes should be fully cooked, and pot should be dry, coating potatoes.

Garnish with chopped chives, Chinese black vinegar and white vinegar powder.

Born in Maryland, **CHEF MICHAEL VOLTAGGIO** began working in restaurants at the age of 15 and hasn't worked outside the industry since. He has studied under several celebrity chefs and the majority of his training has been in fine dining kitchens with an emphasis on modern technique, flavor and presentation. He has been the recipient of several awards including the "AAA 5 Diamond" and "Mobil Award" while serving as Chef de Cuisine at the **Dining Room at The Ritz-Carlton** in Naples, Florida as well as a "Michelin Star" while serving as Chef de Cuisine of Charlie Palmer's **Dry Creek Kitchen** in California. In 2009, he was a finalist for the James Beard Foundation "Best New Restaurant" Award while serving as chef at **The Bazaar** by José Andrés. Michael is the owner/chef of the highly acclaimed restaurant **ink.** and the artisanal sandwich concept **Sack Sandwiches** in Los Angeles. Celebrated having reinterpreted a new class of finer dining at ink., Voltaggio embraces the city's diverse ethnicities, cultures and industries, dubbing the food and experience there as Modern Los Angeles. Michael has also been featured on Bravo's "Top Chef," as winner of season six, and has been recognized as one of *Food & Wine's* Best New Chefs in 2013. Chef Voltaggio supports Alex's Lemonade Stand Foundation by participating in culinary events such as L.A. Loves Alex's Lemonade.

Smoked Blue Catfish Rillettes

JENNIFER CARROLL

Usually, rillettes are made from pork, cooked slowly in fat until it is tender enough to be easily shredded and form a spread-like consistency. Pulling in flavors and influences from the Mediterranean coast of France, this recipe uses the less fatty catfish as a delightful substitute. Serve it with crusty bread on a salad or serve on its own to fully enjoy its smoky tenderness.

SERVES 4 TO 6

¼ log Japanese smoke apple wood (or ¼ cup of apple wood chips)
1 skinless blue catfish fillet, cut into 1" pieces
2 cups dry white wine
2 cups water
1 Tbsp shallot, minced
1 Tbsp garlic, minced
3 oz smoked salmon, cut into ¼" pieces
¼ cup sour cream
¼ cup mayonnaise
¼ cup lemon juice, fresh squeezed
1 Tbsp fresh chive, thinly sliced
1 Tbsp fresh parsley, thinly sliced
½ Tbsp fresh tarragon, thinly sliced
1 tsp fine sea salt
½ tsp white pepper, freshly ground

Set smoke log on fire, blow out flames to just have smoldering embers, then place into a smoker.

Season the catfish fillets with salt and white pepper and smoke for 20 minutes.

While fish is smoking, bring the wine, water, shallot and garlic to a boil in a saucepan over high heat. Reduce to a simmer; add catfish immediately from the smoker. Gently poach until catfish is opaque in the center, about 5 to 7 minutes.

(continued)

Remove catfish from poaching liquid and transfer to a paper towel-lined plate to drain.

Strain poaching liquid through a fine-mesh sieve; discard liquid and set aside garlic and shallot.

Chill the catfish, garlic and shallot completely.

Once chilled, place catfish, garlic, shallot, smoked salmon, sour cream, mayonnaise, chive, parsley and lemon juice in a big bowl and mix gently to break up the catfish.

Season with salt and white pepper.

CHEF JENNIFER CARROLL is executive chef and partner at **Requin**, a seafood-focused French Mediterranean restaurant in Fairfax, Virginia. Carroll was a finalist and fan favorite on the sixth season of Bravo's "Top Chef," and also appeared on "Top Chef: All-Stars," "Top Chef Duels," "Life After Top Chef" and multiple other cooking shows. Prior to moving to the nation's capital, Carroll started her own culinary consulting company, **Carroll Couture Cuisine**, LLC, in 2011, and teamed up with the **Marcus Samuelsson Group** at the **Red Rooster** in Harlem as well as his Bermuda pop-up **Samuelsson**. Carroll served as sous chef at Chef Eric Ripert's prestigious **Le Bernardin** in New York City and was selected by Ripert to lead the kitchen at **10 Arts Bistro & Lounge** when it opened inside The Ritz-Carlton Philadelphia in 2008. Chef Carroll has been actively involved with Alex's Lemonade Stand Foundation since its beginnings when she worked in Philadelphia and is very close to the cause by raising funds and awareness for pediatric cancer. She has participated in The Great Chefs Event in Philadelphia since 2010, as well as Lemon: NYC.

Bacon Wrapped Dates with Parmesan K

SUZANNE GOIN

Each one of these savory dates invokes a range of flavors, from sweet to salty and a hint of smoky. These Parmesan-stuffed bites can easily be prepared ahead of time, put in the oven close to snack time and are irresistible to kids and adults alike.

MAKES 24 DATES

24 deglet noor dates, pitted
¼ lb Parmigiano-Reggiano
24 3" bacon strips, very thinly sliced
5 leaves flat-leaf parsley

Preheat the oven to 400 degrees.

Using a small paring knife, cut a small slit across the length of each date. Cut the cheese into approximately ½" by ¼" rectangles (the cheese will not cut into perfect shapes, but that's OK).

Insert a piece of Parmigiano into each date. Lay the strips of bacon out on a workspace, next to each other. One by one, place each date at the end of a strip of bacon and then carefully roll the date along the bacon strip, wrapping it tightly.

Place the bacon-wrapped dates on a roasting rack set in a rimmed baking sheet and roast for 10 to 15 minutes, until golden brown and crispy on the outside.

Arrange the dates in a bowl with the parsley leaves.

Remember to warn your guests that the dates are hot!

Quick Sauté of Zucchini with Toasted Almonds and Pecorino

JIMMY BRADLEY

A note from Chef Bradley: We've served this dish at The Red Cat since our first dinner back in 1999. It sums up a lot of what I think makes a dish comfortable to both the cook and the diner: a mere handful of ingredients, each contributing its own important flavor and texture, and the whole thing held together with a fine extra virgin olive oil. It's that simple, but the flavor is very complex and complete.

The most important thing here is to not overcook the zucchini. When cooking it, check it with the back of your hand; get it out of the pan when it's warm, but not too hot. Technically speaking, "quick sauté" is redundant; to sauté something means to make it "jump in the pan." But I include quick in the title to emphasize the importance of just barely cooking the zucchini – as soon as it begins to sweat little tears of moisture, get the pan off the burner. This will unlock its flavor and help it meld with those of the almonds and oil.

SERVES 4

¼ cup extra virgin olive oil, plus more for serving
¼ cup almonds, sliced
3 to 4 small zucchini, sliced lengthwise into ⅛" thick slices, then into matchstick-sized segments (about 5 cups matchsticks)
Salt
Black pepper, freshly ground
¼ lb Pecorino Romano, thinly sliced into 12 triangular sheets with an old-fashioned cheese slicer or a very sharp knife

Divide the oil among 2 large, heavy-bottomed skillets and heat it over high heat. When the oil is hot but not smoking, add half the almonds to each pan. Cook, tossing or stirring, until the almonds are golden-brown, approximately 30 seconds.

Add half the zucchini to each pan and toss or stir to coat the zucchini with the hot oil, just a few seconds. Remove the pans from the heat, season with salt and pepper, and return to the heat for 30 seconds, tossing to warm and distribute the seasoning.

Divide the zucchini and almonds among 4 warm salad plates, drizzle with extra virgin olive oil, arrange the pecorino sheets in a pyramid over each serving, and get it to the table while it's still nice and hot.

The author and Chef/Owner of **The Red Cat** **CHEF JIMMY BRADLEY** presides over a neighborhood joint that has become a destination for guests from around New York City and the country. A purveyor of straightforward, occasionally irreverent, food and contagious conviviality, all of it wrapped up in an attitude-free package, Bradley has helped contemporary diners rediscover the intrinsic value of classic Mediterranean cuisine, reinterpreted for a modern American clientele. He and his recipes are regularly featured in *The New York Times, Food & Wine, Bon Appétit, Esquire* and other food publications, as well as on local and national television programs including NBC's "Today," "Top Chef Masters" and "Martha Stewart." His first cookbook, *The Red Cat Cookbook*, was published in 2006. Chef Bradley has participated in The Great Chefs Event and, in his own words, "never misses" the Lemon: NYC culinary event.

Pink Snapper Ceviche with Passion Fruit

JOSE GARCES

A note from Chef Garces: This ceviche is derived from one that my team and I created for an "Iron Chef America" battle in which the secret ingredient was passion fruit and I relied on my knowledge of Peruvian-style ceviche preparation to pull out a winning dish. You can use any firm-fleshed white fish as long as it's supremely fresh. The sauce needs at least an hour to chill but can be made 3 days in advance, stored in the refrigerator.

SERVES 8

To make the passion fruit sauce:

2 tsp garlic (about 2 cloves), minced
1 small shallot, finely diced
2 red Fresno chiles, seeded and minced
¼ cup grapeseed oil
1 qt store-bought passion fruit juice
¼ cup orange juice, freshly squeezed
¼ cup lime juice, freshly squeezed
1 Tbsp agave nectar
1 Tbsp salt

Combine the garlic, shallot, chiles and grapeseed oil in a small saucepan over low heat and cook, stirring often, until the shallots are translucent, about 10 minutes.

Add the passion fruit juice and cook until reduced to 1 ½ cups, 12 to 15 minutes.

Transfer the mixture to a blender and purée until smooth. Add the orange and lime juices and pulse to combine.

Season to taste with 1 Tbsp agave nectar and 1 Tbsp salt. Chill thoroughly before using, at least 1 to 2 hours and up to 3 days (keep in an airtight container).

(continued)

To make the ceviche:

1 lb fresh skinless pink snapper, red snapper or black bass fillet, pin bones removed, diced small
¼ cup extra virgin olive oil
2 small shallots, finely diced
2 red Fresno chiles, thinly slivered
¼ cup chopped fresh cilantro
Kosher salt
2 fresh passion fruits, halved, seeds and pulp scooped out with a spoon and reserved, skin discarded
2 Tbsp black sesame seeds
2 scallions (white and green parts), thinly sliced
Coarse sea salt

Measure out ¼ cup of the passion fruit sauce and combine it in a small bowl with the fish, olive oil, shallots, chiles and cilantro. Season to taste with kosher salt.

Divide the ceviche among eight chilled glass bowls and garnish each portion with some passion fruit seeds and pulp, black sesame seeds, scallion and sea salt.

Pass the remaining passion fruit sauce at the table.

Renowned Latin-American **CHEF JOSE GARCES** translates his rich cultural traditions and culinary vision into personal dining experiences through **Garces**, the eponymous Philadelphia-based hospitality group. Garces operates more than 15 restaurants across the country, including **Amada, Distrito, Tinto, Village Whiskey, Garces Trading Company, JG Domestic, Volvér, Rural Society, The Olde Bar, Buena Onda** and **Mercat a la Planxa** (in partnership with Sage Hospitality). Garces also operates Garces Events, a full-service catering and event division; the Garces Foundation, a philanthropic organization dedicated to Philadelphia's underserved immigrant community; and Luna Farm, Chef Garces' 40-acre farm in Bucks County, PA. Chef Garces has been an avid supporter of Alex's Lemonade Stand Foundation for many years and has participated since the inaugural Great Chefs Event in 2006.

AMADA
JG

Pea Pancakes

BILL TELEPAN

Transform farmers market selections into a fresh, satisfying dish featuring sugar snap peas, in season in the spring.

SERVES 4

To make the pancake:

4 oz sugar snap peas, strings removed
½ cup shelled peas (or substitute frozen peas, thaw but do not cook)
2 Tbsp milk
1 Tbsp cream
1 egg
¼ cup flour
⅛ to ¼ tsp sugar (more if using frozen peas)
¼ tsp salt
½ tsp baking powder
½ tsp butter

Preheat oven to 450 degrees.

Prepare an ice water bath. In lightly salted boiling water, add sugar snap peas and cook 2 minutes. Add to ice water until chilled, about 2 minutes. Strain and set aside.
If using fresh peas, add to same boiling water and cook until just tender, about 2 to 4 minutes depending on size. Transfer to ice water and chill for 2 minutes. Strain and set aside.

In a blender, purée sugar snaps with milk and cream. Transfer to a mixing bowl. Mix in the egg. Add flour, sugar, salt and baking powder. Purée the shell peas in food processor and mix into batter.

Melt ½ tsp butter, in a medium oven-safe non-stick pan over high heat. Swirl butter around pan. Use 2 Tbsp of batter to form a pancake 3" in diameter. Cook two at a time. When the edges start to lightly brown, about 1 to 2 minutes, place in oven for 2 minutes. Flip the pancakes and return to oven until lightly brown, about 4 minutes. Repeat with remaining batter. Keep pancakes warm.

(continued)

To make the topping:

1 lb fresh peas, shell on (1½ cups shelled)
½ lb sugar snap peas, strings removed and cut into 3 pieces on the bias (1½ cups)
3 Tbsp butter
½ cup vegetable stock or water
1 oz pea leaves
2 tsp finely sliced mint
Salt

To prepare the peas, cook for 30 seconds in lightly salted boiling water, remove and place in ice water to chill for 2 minutes. Drain and set aside.

Place snap peas, butter, stock and a pinch of salt in a pot and bring to a boil over high heat. Add the peas and pea leaves and reduce to glaze, about 3 to 5 minutes. Salt to taste and spoon over pancakes.

Sprinkle with sliced mint.

CHEF BILL TELEPAN has been the Executive Chef of Wellness in the Schools (WITS) since 2008, and is Executive Chef of **Oceana**. As the first chef to join the WITS team, Bill has served as a leader of the WITS Cook for Kids program by developing nutritious school menus, training WITS in-residence cooks and cafeteria staff, teaching culinary and nutrition concepts to students, parents and teachers and engaging professional chefs across the country. In 2005, Bill opened **Telepan** restaurant on the Upper West Side. Telepan earned a loyal following and many accolades including a Michelin Star, a glowing two-star review from *The New York Times*, and the title of "Best Newcomer" in the 2007 *Zagat* survey as well as #22 in *Zagat's* "Top 100 Restaurants in NYC 2016." Bill has been a repeat semifinalist for the James Beard Foundation Award for "Best Chef: New York City" and was the recipient of the "Snailblazer Award in 2013" by Slow Food NYC. He has made appearances on NBC's "Today," "Martha Stewart," "CBS This Morning," "Live! with Kelly and Michael," "Rachael Ray" and "The Chew."

Bill is dedicated to helping make people aware that many children suffer every day. By his involvement in Alex's Lemonade Stand Foundation culinary events, such as Lemon: NYC, Bill hopes, "My little part of spreading the word and raising funds enables these kids to have a bright future and help researchers to end cancer."

Burrata with Heirloom Tomatoes

EMILIO MIGNUCCI

A note from Chef Mignucci: This variation on a Caprese salad is a Di Bruno Bros. classic. Serve it with grilled bread, olives and Prosecco for a light appetizer or a summer lunch. It's easily doubled or halved.

SERVES 4

1 lb heirloom tomatoes, cut into bite-size pieces (or about 2 cups halved cherry tomatoes)
8 basil leaves, sliced into ribbons
¾ cup balsamic vinegar
3 Tbsp extra virgin olive oil
2 garlic cloves, minced
Sea salt and freshly ground pepper
2 packages of burrata cheese, about 12 oz each
1 loaf rustic Italian bread, cut into thick slices and grilled or toasted

Toss the tomatoes with the basil and balsamic. While they sit, make a quick garlic oil – just heat the olive oil in a frying pan over medium-high heat for about a minute, then add the minced garlic. You don't want it to brown, so as soon as the garlic begins to sizzle, remove the pan from the burner.

Pour the hot garlic oil over the tomatoes and season with salt and pepper. Arrange the tomato mixture on four plates, and slice the burrata vertically in half. There's cream inside, so make sure you do this on a cutting board or plate. Arrange the halved burrata on top of the tomatoes. Serve with thick slices of grilled or toasted bread.

CHEF EMILIO MIGNUCCI is one of three, third-generation family business owners who currently leads **Di Bruno Bros**, a leading specialty food retailer that originated in Philadelphia's Italian Market. Growing up, Emilio spent the vast majority of his time in the original Di Bruno Bros. 9th Street store, working, tasting and learning all about the delicious imported products that founders Danny and Joe Di Bruno offered in their small shop. The love of food that he developed over the years led Emilio to pursue an Associate's Degree in Culinary Arts. After graduating from the Restaurant School in 1986, he returned to Di Bruno Bros. to take a leadership position as Vice President of Culinary Pioneering. One of Emilio's main responsibilities in his current role is discovering new products and deciding which of them will get a coveted spot on the Di Bruno Bros. shelves. He has been recognized by several organizations for his success in doing so; most notably by the Italian Trade Commission for his representation of Italian Food and Culture and the James Beard Foundation for making Philadelphia a "better food city." He also loves to talk about cheese and spends his time educating members of the restaurant community on the merits of a great cheese plate and how to speak about cheese confidently with their guests.

Emilio's expertise and passion for food has helped him to grow the cheese offerings at Di Bruno Bros. from the 50 varieties it offered in its earlier days to well over 600 cheeses from all over the world. He still works every Saturday at the Italian Market store where it all began and divides the rest of his time between looking for the next great specialty food product, working at the various Di Bruno Bros. locations and contributing to the various boards and committees in which he participates. Regardless of what he may be doing at any given moment, Emilio is always demonstrating Di Bruno Bros.' core value of "Celebrating Great Food, Great People and Great Business." Emilio has participated in several Great Chefs Events as a chef and donated many auction items to the Foundation.

//////

Roasted Mushrooms in Foil K

MARC VETRI

A note from Chef Vetri: Turn to this side dish when you run out of burners on your stove top or when you are cooking outside. You can put the packet of mushrooms on a grill, over a wood fire or in an oven. The oven method is easiest, but if you put them right over a fire, just keep moving the packet around, so the mushrooms don't scorch on the bottom.

SERVES 4 TO 6

1 ¼ lb chanterelle mushrooms, cleaned and halved if small or quartered if large
3 cloves garlic, smashed
4 sprigs rosemary or 6 sprigs thyme
3 Tbsp extra virgin olive oil
1 Tbsp sherry vinegar
Salt and freshly ground pepper

Preheat oven to 450 degrees. Pile the mushrooms on 2 large sheets of aluminum foil, then scatter on the garlic, rosemary, oil and vinegar. Season with salt and pepper to taste.

Fold over the foil and crimp it down tightly over the mushrooms. Pop the packet in an oven and roast until you can hear the mushrooms simmering when you put your ear near the packet, 12 to 15 minutes. Remove the packet from the oven and let stand for 5 to 6 minutes before opening.

Open the packet, remove the herbs, and transfer the mixture to a platter or plates, drizzling the juices over the top.

White Asparagus Soup with Truffled Farm Egg and Green Garlic Puree

NANCY OAKES

A note from Chef Oakes: Few things are more satisfying than poached eggs; we think they are an almost perfect food. But when infused with truffles, satisfying turns into sublime. It would be difficult to choose the star of this dish: elegant white asparagus, poached eggs with earthy truffles or the rich tangy garlic puree. Combined, they create a soulful but sophisticated first course, or all by itself as a light supper or brunch.

SERVES 6

To make the asparagus soup:

2 bunches white asparagus, with ends trimmed
4 cups heavy cream
Salt and pepper
2 shallots, sliced
1 clove garlic, crushed
1 leek, white part only, split, cleaned and sliced
4 sprigs thyme
1 bay leaf
2 Tbsp butter
4 cups white chicken stock

Poach the asparagus in seasoned cream until tender (it should have a slight resistance when pierced with a sharp knife). Cool slightly. Puree asparagus with some of the cream in a blender. Strain and reserve.

In a saucepan, melt the butter and sweat the aromatics and herbs until translucent. Add the stock and simmer for 20 minutes. Strain. Add the stock to the asparagus and cream and check for seasoning.

To make the green garlic puree:

1 bunch curly parsley
1 bunch green garlic, trimmed, split, sliced and washed
1 head garlic, peeled
2 Tbsp butter
¼ cup heavy cream
Salt and pepper

Blanch the parsley in salted water, shock in ice water and drain. Blanch the green garlic in the same water until just tender, shock and drain. Place the garlic cloves in a pot of cold salted water and bring to a simmer. Drain and repeat process three times.

Puree blanched ingredients in a blender with a few ice cubes until a thick puree is achieved.

In a small saucepan, heat the butter and cream and then add the puree and heat through. Season with salt and pepper, reserve.

To make the truffled farm egg:
6 small/medium farm fresh eggs
2 tsp truffle oil mixed with 2 tsp olive oil
½ to 1 oz fresh black truffle, thinly sliced
Coarse gray sea salt and freshly ground black pepper
6 squares of plastic film (12 x 12" approximately)
6 small ramekins or cups, a muffin tin works well

Place the plastic wrap flat on the work surface, brush a 6" circle in the center with the oils. Place ⅙ of the sliced truffle in a circle in the center, overlapping each other. Transfer to the ramekin. Crack the egg and place onto the truffles. Season with coarse salt and pepper.

Gather and twist the plastic up and around the egg leaving a little air space for expansion. In a medium sauté pan filled with 1 ½" of simmering water, place the plastic bundle into the pan and coddle the egg for 4 to 5 minutes until whites are cooked and yolk is still runny.

Unwrap truffled egg, place in the center of a warmed bowl, ladle hot soup around and drizzle with green garlic puree.

In 1993, **CHEF NANCY OAKES** opened **Boulevard** Restaurant with Pat Kuleto. This celebrated establishment has earned Chef Oakes numerous local, national and international accolades, nominations and awards; including Zagat's "San Francisco Bay Area's Most Popular Restaurant," the James Beard Foundation Award for "Best Chef: California" 2001 and "Outstanding Restaurant" 2012, as well as the Filiale des Etats-Unis in France. In 2010, Chef Oakes opened **Prospect** with Pam Mazzola and Kathy King in San Francisco's flourishing South of Market/Embarcadero neighborhood. Chef Nancy Oakes is a pioneer of haute American cuisine. Her unparalleled standard of excellence and accessible, yet groundbreaking, dishes have kept diners returning for decades.

Chef Oakes has been involved with Alex's Lemonade Stand Foundation since 2012 when her culinary friends in Los Angeles asked her to participate in the third annual L.A. Loves Alex's Lemonade event and she has participated annually ever since.

Yucatan Guacamole K

SUE TORRES

A creative spin on traditional Mexican flavors, this recipe uses the citrus from a pineapple to give the dip an added spirit of freshness.

SERVES 4 TO 6

2 ripe avocados
1 Tbsp cilantro, chiffonade
1 Tbsp ginger, diced candied
1 tsp serrano chile, minced
3 Tbsp golden pineapple, diced
½ lime, juiced
1 Tbsp cured red onions
Kosher salt to taste

Halve and pit the avocados and scoop the flesh into a medium bowl with a spoon. Add the lime juice and mix well, using the spoon or a potato masher to break the avocado into small chunks. Stir in the rest of the ingredients. Cover with plastic until ready to serve. Serve with green plantain chips.

CHEF SUE TORRES has been setting the standard for gourmet Mexican fare for over 15 years. She's the Executive Chef at **The Hunt Club**, Fairfield, CT., a consultant for **Leyenda** in Brooklyn, NY and previous owner of **Sueños** in New York City. Over the years, Torres has received notable recognition: *Time Out* named her "Culinary Ambassador" in 2004, and *Working Woman* included her on their list of "20 under 30" to watch. Her innovative dishes and cocktails have earned her much praise from *The New York Times*, *Vogue*, *Food & Wine* and *Bon Appétit*, to mention a few, and have established her as one of the most revered chefs in New York. Torres' original recipes have been featured in several national magazines, including *Fine Cooking* and *Food & Wine*. She is also a top-notch restaurant consultant and a genuinely committed philanthropist working with charity groups that include the Cystic Fibrosis Foundation, Autism Speaks and Women Breast & Ovarian Cancer. Torres has also been featured on Bravo's "Top Chef Masters." Chef Torres has supported Alex's Lemonade Stand Foundation by participating in The Great Chefs Event in Philadelphia.

Tomato, Mayonnaise, Basil and Toast

TYLER FLORENCE

Ideal for a weekend brunch, sweet and juicy tomatoes are the star here. When in season, visit the farmers market for the freshest flavors. Chef Florence suggests that when using Roma tomatoes, before slicing them cut off ¼" from the stem end and use a small spoon to remove the seed clusters (known as "tomato caviar") and use them for garnish.

SERVES 4

To make the mayonnaise:

2 egg whites
¼ tsp Dijon mustard
2 tsp fresh lemon juice
¼ tsp kosher salt
¼ tsp sugar
1 cup grapeseed oil

In a blender, combine the egg whites, mustard, lemon juice, salt and sugar. Blend until smooth. With the blender running, add the grapeseed oil in a slow, steady stream so the mixture emulsifies. Refrigerate until ready to serve.

To prepare the tomatoes:

1 lb assorted heirloom, Roma and cherry tomatoes
Extra virgin olive oil
Flaky sea salt
Freshly cracked black pepper
4 thick slices sourdough bread
Small fresh basil leaves

Cut the larger tomatoes into small wedges and bite-size pieces. Slice the Roma tomatoes. Heat 2" of olive oil to 375 degrees in a large pot. Place the cherry tomatoes in a wire mesh skimmer and submerge it in the hot oil for 2 to 3 seconds, just until the skins burst. Remove from the oil and season with flaky sea salt. Toss the cherry tomatoes with the other tomatoes. Dress with a little olive oil and season with a turn of cracked black pepper.

Preheat a gas or charcoal grill or grill pan. Drizzle olive oil over the bread slices and grill for 1 minute per side until crispy and charred around the edges, but still soft in the middle. Serve the tomatoes on the grilled bread with olive oil and dots of the mayonnaise; garnish with the reserved tomato caviar and fresh basil.

Reprinted with permission from Tyler Florence FRESH *by Tyler Florence.*

After over 20 years as a Food Network star, **CHEF TYLER FLORENCE** has captivated millions of viewers on numerous hit shows, including: "Tyler's Ultimate", his signature series; "The Great Food Truck Race," a #1 series for the network; "How to Boil Water," a cooking show for novices; and "Food 911," his hugely popular recipe rescue show. In 2008, Tyler opened **Tyler Florence Fresh** at San Francisco International Airport, followed in 2010 by **Wayfare Tavern** in San Francisco's Financial District. In 2011, Tyler was awarded "Restaurateur of the Year" by *Wine Enthusiast Magazine* and both of his restaurants were awarded three-star reviews from *San Francisco Chronicle* restaurant critic, Michael Bauer. He also has his own line of award-winning wines sourced from world-class California vineyards. Tyler Florence Wines have received over 29 awards and ratings, including a 92-point rating for his first TF Zin. Tyler has authored multiple best-selling books including *Tyler Florence Test Kitchen*, *Tyler Makes a Birthday Cake*, *Tyler Makes Spaghetti & Tyler Makes Pancakes*, *Start Fresh: Your Child's Jump Start to Lifelong Healthy Eating* and *Family Meal*. Chef Florence has participated in the Lemon: NYC culinary event, benefitting Alex's Lemonade Stand Foundation.

Crispy Polenta Fries with Spicy Ketchup K

MICHAEL SCHWARTZ

A note from Chef Schwartz: Polenta fries are a kind of a strange concept when you think about it, but that's probably why they make so much sense! These golden and crispy sticks are cheesy and creamy on the inside and served stacked like Jenga with salsa-ed up ketchup for dunking. Whether you're a kid or a grown-up, you have to smile because polenta fries are not only deliciously addictive, they're fun to eat.

MAKES 2 DOZEN

To make the polenta fries:

1 qt whole milk, preferably organic
2 Tbsp unsalted butter
2 cups yellow cornmeal (not quick cooking), medium grind
1 cup Grana Padano or Parmesan cheese, grated
Kosher salt
Freshly ground black pepper
Canola oil, for frying

Line a 13" x 9" baking dish with plastic wrap, letting excess hang over the sides. Set aside.

Bring the milk, 1 cup water and butter to a simmer over medium heat in a large pot. Gradually whisk in the cornmeal in a slow steady stream. Reduce the heat to medium-low and switch to a wooden spoon. Cook, stirring often until the polenta is very thick and pulls away from sides of pot, about 15 minutes. Remove from the heat. Stir in the cheese until incorporated; season with 1 tsp salt and ½ tsp pepper.

Pour the polenta into the prepared baking dish, spreading evenly with a rubber spatula; it should be about ½" thick. Refrigerate until completely cool and firm, at least 1 hour or even better overnight. It's important that the polenta sets up completely and gets quite dense, so it's easy to cut into strips that won't fall apart in the hot oil when you fry them.

Heat 3" of oil to 350 degrees in a countertop electric fryer or deep pot. If you don't have a deep-fry thermometer, a good way to test if the oil is hot enough is to stick the end of a wooden spoon or a chopstick in it, if bubbles circle around the end then you're good to go.

(continued)

Grab the ends of the plastic wrap and lift the polenta out of the baking dish and onto a cutting board. Flip the polenta over to remove the plastic. Cut the polenta into thirds and then crosswise into sticks. You should wind up with 24 large Lincoln Log-like pieces, approximately ¾" wide by 4" long.

Put the polenta sticks in a fryer basket or spider strainer and carefully lower into the hot oil; do this in batches to avoid overcrowding and to keep the oil temperature constant. Fry the polenta sticks for 3 to 5 minutes, until they are golden brown and crispy, removing the cooked ones to a paper towel-lined platter to drain before adding the next batch. Season lightly with salt while the fries are still hot. Stack the polenta fries like Lincoln Logs on a large platter. Serve with spicy ketchup.

MAKES 2 CUPS

To make the spicy ketchup:
1 Tbsp vegetable oil
½ small onion, coarsely chopped
2 garlic cloves, coarsely chopped
1 jalapeño, seeded and chopped
Kosher salt
Freshly ground black pepper
2 cups ketchup
1 Tbsp chopped fresh cilantro

Place a small skillet over medium heat. When the pan is hot, coat with the oil. Add the onion, garlic and jalapeño; season with salt and pepper. Stir until the onions soften and start to take on a little color, about 3 minutes.

Scrape the vegetable mixture into a food processor. Pulse until combined but not totally smooth; you want to keep the chunky texture. Transfer to a bowl and add the ketchup and cilantro. Mix together until well blended; season again with salt and pepper if necessary.

CHEF MICHAEL SCHWARTZ is the owner of **The Genuine Hospitality Group**, a James Beard Foundation Award winner, the face of the South Florida restaurant industry and a nationally recognized celebrity chef. Honored with the prestigious James Beard Foundation Award for "Best Chef: South" in 2010, Schwartz is recognized by his peers and the diners that flock to his restaurants for his commitment to the community and responsible seasonal food sourcing. Outside of the restaurant, Schwartz focuses his time and influence supporting the arts and causes such as Share our Strength, Alex's Lemonade Stand Foundation, Slow Food (from which he received its Miami convivium's first "Snail of Approval") and Wellness in the Schools. The chef's cookbook, *MICHAEL'S GENUINE FOOD: Down-to-Earth Cooking for People Who Love to Eat* features beloved recipes, a homage to approachable, sensible and affordable food that everyone loves to make and eat. His recipes and restaurants have been covered by *The New York Times*, *The Wall Street Journal*, *Food & Wine*, *Travel + Leisure*, NBC's "Today" and more.

Chef Schwartz is a regular at many Alex's Lemonade Stand Foundation culinary events. Says Schwartz, "I think what's always blown me away about Alex's Lemonade Stand Foundation is the pure joy that everyone involved brings to the table. It's a beautiful thing to have a community of chefs backing a cause and having fun doing it. I know I'm not alone when I say The Great Chefs Event is the one I look forward to most all year."

Carrot Soup with Toasted Marshmallow K

KEVIN SBRAGA

When the air becomes crisp, and you are looking for something cozy, this carrot soup is the perfect fix. With a touch ginger, Chef Sbraga serves this soup garnished with toasted marshmallows and a pistachio oil drizzle. Consider this a new addition to your traditional holiday dishes.

SERVES 6 TO 10

2 Thai chile peppers
2 shallots
47 oz carrots
31 oz ginger
5 oz sherry
7 oz honey
1 qt vegetable stock
2 qt heavy cream

Using a large pot or Dutch oven, sauté the vegetables over medium heat. Add the sherry and continue cooking until reduced by half.

Add the honey, vegetable stock and heavy cream. Simmer for 45 minutes.

Remove from heat and allow to cool. Using an immersion blender, blend on high until smooth.

Salt to taste.

Garnish with toasted marshmallow and pistachio oil drizzle.

CHEF KEVIN SBRAGA is Chef/Owner of **Sbraga Dining**, including **Sbraga**, **The Fat Ham University City** and **The Fat Ham King of Prussia**. In 2008, he began consulting work with Jose Garces to test recipes for the chef-proprietor's *Latin Evolution* cookbook. Sbraga impressed Garces with his dedication, which earned him a full-time role as Culinary Director of Garces Restaurant Group. Sbraga went on to win the award for "Best Meat Presentation" in the Bocuse d'Or USA competition in 2008, before working as Executive Chef for Stephen Starr at **Rat's Restaurant** at the Grounds for Sculpture in New Jersey. In 2010, Sbraga joined the cast of "Top Chef," emerging from the season with the win and a zest for opening his own concept. He launched modern American restaurant Sbraga in Philadelphia in 2011, which has since been named an *Esquire* "Best New Restaurant" in 2012 and one of *Philadelphia Magazine's* "Best Restaurants" on a yearly basis. Sbraga's second, critically-acclaimed venture, The Fat Ham, opened in 2013 in the University City neighborhood of Philadelphia. A second location opened in King of Prussia, PA in 2016. Chef Sbraga has supported Alex's Lemonade Stand Foundation since 2014 by participating annually in The Great Chefs Event.

Roasted Carrots with Dill Salsa Verde

HILLARY STERLING

Don't let the simplicity of this dish fool you - these roasted carrots are packed full of flavor. The fresh dill is the perfect complement to this springtime side dish.

SERVES 2

To make the roasted carrots:

5 to 7 baby carrots
3 sprigs of thyme
2 shallots
½ orange, juiced
Red wine vinegar
Olive oil
Salt
Fennel pollen

Toss baby carrots with salt, olive oil and thyme to coat. Place on a sheet tray and roast at 475 degrees until tender.

Roast shallots, halve skin on, season with olive oil and salt, place either on a grill or hot pan until charred then place in bowl with plastic wrap and steam until tender. Peel skin and petal the shallot. Dress in red wine vinegar and olive oil.

Warm carrots in sauté pan, dress with 1 Tbsp red wine vinegar and the juice of half an orange.

Top with 1 heaping Tbsp of dill salsa verde, 5 capers, 3 petals of roasted marinated shallots, a sprinkle of fennel pollen and garnish with dill and carrot tops.

(continued)

To make the dill salsa verde:

1 bunch dill, washed and finely chopped
1 bunch carrot tops, washed and finely chopped
1 shallot, brunoise
4 cloves of garlic, minced
2 filets of anchovies, minced
1 Tbsp capers, rinsed and chopped
3 eggs, 3 minute cooked yolks
1 cup olive oil
3 Tbsp red wine vinegar, added when ready to serve

Combine ingredients in a blender or food processor. Pulse to a thick but pourable consistency.

CHEF HILLARY STERLING is the chef at **Vic's**, a new neighborhood Italian-Mediterranean restaurant in New York City from Victoria Freeman and Marc Meyer. In 2014, Sterling was introduced to Freeman and Meyer, and found their market-driven approach in keeping with her ethos. The modern, airy aesthetic of Vic's is reflected in Sterling's approachable menu of thoughtfully prepared Italian dishes, such as oyster mushrooms with potato, botarga and lemon and sheep's milk agnolotti with hazelnut. Building on the innate principals of Italian cooking, she sources ingredients locally—from finishing salt that is made in Hell's Kitchen to flour ground in New York State—and lets her menu be guided by the seasons. Chef Sterling has participated in Alex's Lemonade Stand Foundation culinary events such as Lemon: NYC and Lemon: Chicago.

Kona Kampachi Tartare with Avocado Mousse

MARC FORGIONE

A note from Chef Forgione: This appetizer has been on our menu from the beginning, and is one of our most popular dishes. Despite the long list of ingredients, it's actually very easy to make. It not only looks impressive - it tastes absolutely incredible, too. I remember playing around with different flavors and textures while I was creating the dish, and while I loved what I was getting as a result, it still wasn't perfect on my palate. One day while looking for something to finish the dish, I noticed a small mound of leftover toasted pine nuts lying around. And me being me, I just thought, "Why not?" I threw the nuts in and tried it - it tasted absolutely perfect. Exactly the missing piece I was looking for. The smokiness from the toasting, the sweetness that the pine nuts are known for and their fattiness were all perfect complements for the fish, avocado and spicy lime sauce.

SERVES 4

To make the sauce:

¼ cup extra virgin olive oil
2 Tbsp teriyaki sauce
1 Tbsp mustard oil
¼ cup mild honey
¼ cup fresh lime juice
Kosher salt
Freshly ground black pepper

Combine the olive oil, teriyaki sauce, mustard oil, honey and lime juice in a small bowl. Season to taste with salt and pepper. Refrigerate until ready to serve.

To make the avocado mousse:

1 avocado, halved and pitted
2 Tbsp fresh lime juice
2 Tbsp extra virgin olive oil
4 to 6 dashes green Tabasco sauce
Kosher salt

Place the avocados, lime juice, olive oil, Tabasco and salt to taste into a blender and puree on the highest speed until smooth. You may need to use the bottom of a ladle to get everything started. Transfer to a nonreactive container, cover and refrigerate until ready to serve.

To make the tartare:
10 oz large-dice kampachi
3 Tbsp extra virgin olive oil
2 Tbsp brunoise cucumbers
Kosher salt
½ cup diced avocados
1 tsp fresh lime juice
1 Tbsp extra virgin olive oil

In a medium bowl, combine the fish, olive oil, cucumber and salt to taste. In another bowl, combine the diced avocado, lime juice (to keep it from oxidizing), and olive oil. Season to taste with salt and set aside.

Place 1 oz of the diced avocado on the bottom of a 2" ring mold. Fill the mold with 2.5 oz of the fish, packing the fish tightly. Repeat with the remaining avocado and tartare—you should fill 4 molds. Transfer the ring molds to a tray and refrigerate until ready to use.

To assemble the dish:
¼ cup pine nuts
4 red radishes, julienned
Micro cilantro
4 (1x¼") sashimi-style slices kampachi
Olive oil
Lime juice
Potato chips
Szechuan buttons

When ready to serve, in a small dry skillet, toast the pine nuts over low heat, periodically shaking the pan to prevent the nuts from burning, until golden and fragrant, about 3 minutes. Transfer to a small bowl and let the nuts cool completely.

Unmold the tartare into chilled bowls by inverting the molds over the bowls. You will have the tartare on the bottom and diced avocado on top. Pour enough of the sauce to come a quarter of the way up the molded tartare. Garnish with the julienned radish and micro cilantro and scatter the toasted pine nuts around.

(continued)

For each bowl of tartare, place a quenelle of the avocado mousse on a large soup spoon and top with a slice of the kampachi. Drizzle with olive oil and lime juice and garnish with a sprig of micro cilantro and a piece of radish. Place a few potato chips on the side of the bowl.

Divide the Szechuan buttons among 4 Asian soup spoons and serve with the bowls of tartare and avocado mousse. Before eating, place the Szechuan bud under your tongue and wait until your mouth begins to "pop" before eating the dish.

CHEF MARC FORGIONE is the chef/owner of the **Restaurant Marc Forgione**, **American Cut** and **Lobster Press** and the co-owner/partner of **Khe-Yo**. He began his career at the age of 16, joining his father, Larry Forgione (a culinary legend who revolutionized American-style cooking in the '70s and '80s), in the kitchen at **An American Place**. Marc fully embraced his father's livelihood and has built on his unique culinary foundation to carve out an identity of his own. After studying at the University of Massachusetts, Marc left for France, where he secured a series of posts under Michel Guerard in Eugenie les Bains.

When he returned to New York, Marc promptly served as chef de cuisine at **BLT Prime**. The restaurant would go on to earn sterling accolades from relevant publications nationwide, culminating in a 27 in the *Zagat Guide*, making it the highest-ranking steakhouse in the history of New York City. Following his role as chef de cuisine, Marc was named corporate chef for the **BLT Restaurant Group**, a position that enabled him to develop recipes and maintain the quality of the BLT brand as it went on to include more restaurants across the country. Marc has played a key role in the openings of **BLT Fish** and **BLT Market**.

Forgione has created an approachable place with partner Christopher Blumlo "that people walk by and are compelled to enter and where the ingredients are the star." Restaurant Marc Forgione was awarded its first Michelin star in 2010. The restaurant also earned the distinction of a two-star *The New York Times* review, was named "Key Newcomer" by *Zagat Guide 2009*, "Top 25 Restaurants in NYC" by *Modern Luxury* magazine and "All Star Eatery" by *Forbes* magazine. Marc Forgione was awarded "Star Chefs Rising Star of the Year Award 2010" named "Rising Star 2008" from *Restaurant Hospitality* magazine and mentioned "New Formalist" by *Esquire* magazine in 2008. In 2010, he was crowned the winner of the "Next Iron Chef" TV show on The Food Network. Chef Forgione has supported Alex's Lemonade Stand Foundation by participating in the Lemon: NYC culinary event.

COCKTAILS & MOCKTAILS

Weekend Warrior

NEAL BODENHEIMER

A note from mixologist Neal Bodenheimer: Baking chocolate, vanilla and roasted corn are only a few of the notes you'll get in this nod to the 20th century cocktail.

SERVES 1

⅗ oz Mellow Corn Bonded Corn Whiskey
¾ oz Mezcal Vago Elote Mezcal
¾ oz Fresh Grapefruit Juice
½ oz Marie Brizard White Creme de Cacao
½ oz Tempus Fugit Kina l'Avion d'Or
7 drops Bittermens Grapefruit Bitters (in tin)

Add liquid ingredients into a shaking tin and shake without ice.

Strain mixture into a Double Old Fashioned Glass with cracked ice.

Use 7 drops Bittermens Bitters for garnish & aromatics atop the drink.

Twist a grapefruit peel and garnish.

Born in New Orleans, **NEAL BODENHEIMER** began working in a bar at age 18. After graduating from the University of Texas at Austin, he embarked on a year-long trip around the world with a focus on exploring food and beverage traditions. Hungry to get back to the states and start working, Neal moved to New York City where he worked for Steve Hanson's B.R. Guest Corporation and Danny Meyer's Union Square Hospitality. After Hurricane Katrina, Neal felt the call back home to New Orleans where he opened the craft cocktail bar **CURE** in 2009, which has been nationally and internationally recognized as one of the best cocktail bars in New Orleans and in the country. CURE has been a James Beard Foundation's "Best Bar Program" semi-finalist in 2013, 2014 and 2016.

In 2012, Neal and his partners opened **Bellocq** at The Hotel Modern in New Orleans. Bellocq, an exploration of 19th century drinks with a focus on aromatized and fortified wines, was named one of *Food & Wine* magazine's "Best New Bars in America" in 2012 and *Esquire's* "Best Bars in America" in 2013. In 2012, Neal and his partners purchased an existing bar and restaurant in the historic Vieux Carre of New Orleans which developed into a new restaurant project, **Cane & Table**. With a focus on rum and proto-tiki cocktails and Caribbean culinary traditions, the restaurant and bar opened in 2013. In just over two years, Cane & Table has been named as one of the "Best Bars in America" by *Food & Wine*, *Esquire* Television, *Eater*, *Thrillist* and one of the "Best New Bars in the South" by *Garden & Gun* and *Southern Living*. Cane & Table also garnered a semi-finalist nomination for the James Beard Foundation's "Best Bar Program" in 2015. Bodenheimer has been a supporter of Alex's Lemonade Stand Foundation since 2010 and has participated in The Great Chefs Event. He has served as a guest mixologist for L.A. Loves Alex's Lemonade and The Great Chefs Event.

Pina's Limoncello

JEFF MICHAUD

Use this delicious recipe to make your own cocktails, but make sure to save some for Jeff's Limoncello Tiramisu recipe, featured in the Desserts section.

MAKES 2 ½ QUARTS

20 Eureka lemons, 15 Sicilian lemons, or 10 Amalfitano lemons
1 qt grain alcohol or 100-proof vodka
5 cups granulated sugar

Peel the lemons, using a vegetable peeler or large zester, taking care not to remove much of the bitter white membrane beneath the peel. Marinate the peels in the grain alcohol in a glass jug at room temperature for 2 weeks. Strain into a pitcher and reserve the peels. Combine the sugar, 1 ½ quarts water and reserved peels in a large saucepan. Bring to a simmer over medium heat, stirring just until the sugar dissolves, 5 to 8 minutes. Remove from the heat and let cool, and then strain out and discard the peels.

Let the syrup cool completely then stir into the alcohol. Store in bottles in the freezer, sipping or using as needed.

Reprinted with permission from Eating Italy: A Culinary Adventure *by Jeff Michaud.*

A nationally recognized chef and author, **JEFF MICHAUD** began his cooking career at the age of 13 at a pizza shop in his native New Hampshire. Inspired by his grandmother's cooking and beautiful homemade wedding cakes, Michaud enrolled in the Culinary Institute of America and graduated in 1998. Upon graduation, Michaud moved to Aspen, CO to join the kitchen staff at the **Caribou Club** where he worked his way up to Executive Sous Chef. After completing his tenure in Aspen, Michaud moved to Philadelphia to work as sous chef for critically acclaimed Chef Marc Vetri at his eponymous restaurant, **Vetri Ristorante**. Discovering his love for Italian cuisine in the Vetri kitchen, Michaud decided to move to Bergamo, Italy to further hone his skills.

After serving as **Locanda del Bianocspino**'s opening chef, Michaud returned to the United States where he took several chef's positions throughout New England before returning to Philadelphia to rejoin the Vetri Family and open **Osteria** in 2007. In 2008, The James Beard Foundation nominated Osteria for "Best New Restaurant" and in 2010, Michaud won the James Beard Foundation Award for "Best Chef: Mid-Atlantic."

In 2013, Michaud published his first cookbook, *Eating Italy: A Culinary Adventure*, that chronicled the intertwining stories of discovering his passion for Italian cuisine and falling in love with his wife, Claudia.

Michaud is currently a member of the Vetri Community Partnership's Board of Directors. Additionally, he has participated in The Great Chefs Event since its inception along with Marc Vetri and Jeff Benjamin.

Green Goddess

CHRISTIAAN ROLLICH

A note from mixologist Christiaan Rollich: This drink originally started as a non-alcoholic cocktail made for a celebrity fundraiser. The day before the event, a client asked me, "You know what would be nice? To have a refreshing non-alcoholic green cocktail for the daytime. Not a lemonade, not a juice, nothing that seems too healthy." I immediately said, "Of course, I can do that." The next day, I walked in the event with 10 gallons of a green non-alcoholic beverage and handed it to Jessica Goin, sister of Chef Suzanne Goin, and head of Lucques Catering. She named the drink Green Goddess after a nickname the press gave her sister when Suzanne started getting recognition as a chef in Los Angeles, as praise for the farm-to-table movement she was making famous in Los Angeles. That was the first time we sold out of a non-alcoholic drink at an event!

When we opened a.o.c., they asked to put it on the cocktail menu and "add some vodka to it." However, when you add spirit to anything it will change the flavor profile, so I revisited the recipe. Since we made everything from scratch, we are not able to pre-batch anything because over time it turns brown. I thought, "What if I infuse the vodka with green tea?" The result was fine, but it needed that next layer. Coating the glass with absinthe worked great. When people read the description, they are a little doubtful. But when they taste the drink, they order a second one. The biggest question of every cocktail maker when you finish your cocktail is, "Would the customer order a second?"

SERVES 1

To make the arugula simple syrup:
1 ½ cups sugar
1 cup water
1 ½ cups loosely packed arugula

Combine the sugar and water in a small saucepan over high heat; let it come to a boil. Once the sugar has dissolved, reduce the heat to medium-low; cook for 10 minutes, then turn off the heat and let the mixture cool to room temperature.

Transfer to a blender, along with the arugula. Puree for 20 seconds, then strain through a fine-mesh strainer into a container with a tight-fitting lid. Discard the solids. Refrigerate until ready to use (up to 3 days). The yield is about 1 cup.

To make the green-tea-infused vodka:
1 cup unflavored vodka
½ tsp green tea leaves (from loose dried tea leaves, not from a tea bag)

Combine the vodka and green tea leaves in a blender. Puree (or highest speed) for about 20 seconds, then strain through a fine-mesh strainer or coffee filter set over a container with a tight-fitting lid. The yield is 1 cup.

To make the cocktail:

Absinthe, for the glass (optional)
1 oz fresh lemon juice
½ oz fresh cucumber juice
Fresh jalapeño juice
Ice cubes
3 thin cucumber slices (unpeeled), for garnish
1 large mint sprig, for garnish

If desired, pour a splash of absinthe into a Tom Collins glass and swirl to coat the inside, then pour it out. Fill the glass with ice cubes.

Combine ¾ oz of the arugula simple syrup, 2 oz of the green-tea-infused vodka, the lemon juice, cucumber juice and a dash or two (to taste) of the jalapeño, deseeded and juiced, in a cocktail shaker. Seal, shake vigorously and strain into the glass.

Garnish: Working with one at a time, gently bend each cucumber slice, then skewer it with an oversize cocktail toothpick so that all 3 slices together create a looping ribbon-like effect. Lay the toothpick across the rim of the glass. Add the mint sprig and straw. Serve right away.

Variation: For a non-alcoholic version of this drink, omit the infused vodka and use 2 ½ oz of chilled green tea instead.

CHRISTIAAN ROLLICH heads the cocktail program for **The Lucques Group** in Los Angeles (**Lucques**, **a.o.c**. and **Tavern**), creating next-level hand-mixed cocktails. As a supporter of Alex's Lemonade Stand Foundation, Christiaan was a guest mixologist at the L.A. Loves Alex's Lemonade event.

Lemon Mojito

DR. JOHN MARIS

Mojitos are a traditional Cuban highball that consists of five ingredients: white rum, sugar, lime juice, soda water and mint. This recipe adds a twist of fresh lemon for a combination of sweetness, refreshing citrus and mint flavors to make this a perfect summer drink.

SERVES 6

¼ cup white sugar
12 sprigs fresh mint
1 lemon, thinly sliced
1 ¼ cups fresh lemon juice
1 cup white rum
1 cup crushed ice
Soda water, chilled, to serve

Divide the sugar and half the mint among 6 serving glasses. Use a fork to crush the mint into the sugar.

Divide the lemon and remaining mint among the glasses.

Combine the lemon juice and rum in a large jug. Pour the lemon juice mixture among the glasses. Top with ice and soda water. Serve immediately.

K For a kid-friendly mocktail, omit the rum to make an old-fashioned lemonade with a hint of mint.

JOHN M. MARIS, MD, is a pediatric oncologist at The Children's Hospital of Philadelphia (CHOP), co-head of the Pediatric Cancer Dream Team and holds the Giulio D'Angio Chair in Neuroblastoma Research. He also serves as chairman of the Children's Oncology Group Neuroblastoma Committee, a research consortium of more than 200 member institutions. Additionally, he serves on the Alex's Lemonade Stand Foundation Scientific Advisory Board, which carefully selects research projects to fund, vetting applications to make sure that ALSF supports the most substantive and critical contributions to the field of childhood cancer research. Dr. Maris was one of the doctors that treated Alex Scott at CHOP when she was undergoing treatment for neuroblastoma.

Alex's Dad's Lemonade

MAX SEAMAN & ERIC ALPERIN

SERVES 12 TO 16

25 oz (1-750ml) moderately peated blended Scotch such as Old Bank Note or Black Grouse
5.5 g (about 2 teabags) English Breakfast tea
5 oz lemon juice
5 oz honey syrup
12 oz Club soda
Lemon wheels and nutmeg (optional) for garnish

Combine 3 parts honey with 1 part very hot water and let cool to make honey syrup.

Steep tea in Scotch for 15 minutes or to taste.

Combine tea-infused Scotch with lemon and honey syrup in a punch bowl. Add a large block of ice and stir to chill. Add 12 oz of chilled club soda. Adjust lemon, honey and club soda to taste (most people will like a little more club soda). Add a little freshly grated nutmeg if desired. Float lemon wheels in punchbowl for garnish.

ERIC ALPERIN & MAX SEAMAN both contribute to **The Varnish**, part of Los Angeles' celebrated 213 Hospitality Inc. The Varnish features meticulously constructed cocktails made with passion and precision by some of the city's most lauded bartenders. In 2012, The Varnish won the prestigious title of "Best American Cocktail Bar" at the Tales of the Cocktail Spirited Awards. Alperin and Seaman have participated as guest mixologists for L.A. Loves Alex's Lemonade.

//////

Dark Rabbit

MARCOS TELLO

SERVES 1

2 oz El Silencio Espadin
½ oz agave nectar
½ oz fresh lime juice
½ oz carrot juice
½ oz celery juice

Build all ingredients in a tiki mug, pilsner glass or swizzle with crushed ice. Garnish with a carrot top or lime wheel with Tajin.

MARCOS TELLO became enamored with the bartender trade while watching his favorite television show, "Cheers", as a young boy growing up in Los Angeles. He developed a fascination with the relationships that formed around the iconic bar — an impression that continues to drive his work today as one of the most acclaimed bartenders in Los Angeles. Tello has received international acclaim for his expertise in prominent publications including *The Los Angeles Times, The New York Times, Food & Wine, GQ,* and *Bon Appétit.*

Tello teamed up with friend and longtime business associate, Aidan Demarest to form **Tello-Demarest Liquid Assests**, a beverage program consultation firm and also heads up the cocktail department of the **Hospitality Collective**, a full service restaurant consultation group. Tello is additionally the founder and chairman of craft-guild, The Sporting Life, and Treasurer of the Los Angeles Chapter of the United States Bartenders Guild. Tello has participated as a guest mixologist at the L.A. Loves Alex's Lemonade culinary event.

Sgroppino Julep

JEFF BENJAMIN

Sgroppino is a mixed drink originating in Venice. Its base is lemon sorbet with vodka topped up with the Italian sparkling wine Prosecco. This recipe brings the essence of Italy to the horse races by transforming it into a julep just by adding Bourbon. Alex's Lemonade Stand Foundation has a long history with horse racing, starting in 2005 when the owners of thoroughbred racehorse, Afleet Alex, invited Alex's mom and dad to set up a lemonade stand at the Kentucky Derby. A few weeks later, Afleet Alex won the Preakness Stakes, despite a dramatic stumble, and brought more attention to the story of Alex Scott.

SERVES 1

1 cup lemon water ice or lemon sorbet
10 oz Prosecco
3 oz Bourbon
1 tsp lemon zest

Scoop water ice into a bowl or martini shaker.

Pour the bourbon over the water ice and whisk together gently until blended but without melting the ice.

Pour the mixture into a white wine glass. Pour Prosecco into the glass, then zest lemon into the glass and enjoy!

Following graduation from the University of Massachusetts-Amherst, **JEFF BENJAMIN** landed in New York City with food service industry giant, Aramark. He spent the better part of the next decade managing high-level corporate employees and executive dining operations. During his time in the Big Apple, Benjamin met and became friends with Chef Marc Vetri. When Vetri decided to return to Philadelphia to open his own restaurant, he enlisted Benjamin to be his general manager.

In 1998, Vetri and Benjamin opened **Vetri Ristorante**, an intimate fine dining restaurant in Philadelphia's Center City neighborhood. Vetri was an instant hit that earned universal acclaim. Within two years of its debut, Vetri received the *Philadelphia Inquirer's* highest restaurant rating and Jeff was made a partner and this dynamic duo has been rolling along ever since. With Vetri and Benjamin at the helm, the Vetri Family continues to grow as a national brand with their new partners, URBN, Inc.

Outside of the restaurants, Benjamin is a committed philanthropist. In 2009, he and Vetri created the Vetri Community Partnership. The organization's signature initiative, "Eatiquette," is a school lunch improvement program that currently serves the Philadelphia and Austin areas. Additionally, Vetri and Benjamin are the founders of The Great Chefs Event, which brings together scores of the country's greatest chefs to raise money and awareness for Alex's Lemonade Stand Foundation and Vetri Community Partnership.

In 2015, Benjamin published his first book, *Front of the House: Restaurant Manners, Misbehaviors & Secrets* which pulls back the curtain to depict all of the behind-the-scenes details that go into an evening out. Benjamin lives in Cherry Hill, NJ, with his wife, Melissa, and their two daughters. When he's not working, he can be found rooting for his children's sports team, and his beloved Cubs and 76ers.

Boulevardier

NAREN YOUNG

A note from mixologist Naren Young: I have this niche and love for all things involving food. Working in a restaurant-bar is harder than working in a regular bar because there's so much more information you need to know. I thrive on the more culinary aspect of the job - I think that's what I enjoy most. Going to farmers markets, talking to chefs, reading food blogs—its all allowed me to be a better bartender and, in turn, a better teacher.

SERVES 1

1 oz Elijah Craig 'Small Batch'
¾ oz Luxardo Bitter
¾ oz Dolin Rouge vermouth

Combine ingredients. Stir and strain on ice. Serve in an etched rocks glass.

Garnish with an orange twist and a plastic stirrer.

With a little bit of cocktail inspiration courtesy of Tom Cruise (no joke), **NAREN YOUNG** started studying classic cocktails at the tender age of 16—which is even two years' shy of his native Australia's generous drinking age. But Young wasn't diving into drink with teenage rebellion. Since taking his first dram of the industry, he has built a nearly 20-year, globe-spanning and multifaceted hospitality career. Young's native and varied skills have taken him around the world, from training bartenders and consulting in Singapore, Argentina, Germany, Brazil and New Zealand (and of course his Ozzie homeland) to tending bar at some of the world's finest cocktail establishments in Sydney, most notably the iconic **Bayswater Brasserie** at the height of its success, as well as bars and restaurants in London and New York, where Young was most recently behind the bar of **The Dutch**.

Young is also a widely published food and drinks journalist. He was nominated again this year as one of the top four drinks writers in the world at the prestigious Tales of the Cocktail Awards in New Orleans. He is often quoted in the media and has made many appearances on television both in Australia and the United States, working with the likes of Martha Stewart, Emeril Lagasse, the Food Network and NBC. Young has been a supporter of Alex's Lemonade Stand Foundation since 2015, serving as a guest mixologist at The Great Chefs Event in Philadelphia.

Melissa's Orange-Raspberry Lemonade K

MELISSA D'ARABIAN

YIELDS JUST OVER 1 QT

4 cups water
¾ cup sugar
¾ cup fresh lemon juice
½ cup freshly-squeezed orange juice
½ cup ice cubes
½ cup frozen raspberries

In a small saucepan, bring 1 cup of water and the sugar to a boil; simmer and stir until the sugar is dissolved, about 2 minutes. Remove from the heat and let the syrup cool completely.

In a pitcher, mix lemon juice, orange juice, cooled syrup and remaining 3 cups of water. Add the ice cubes and frozen raspberries. Stir and serve.

Celebrity chef, television host, best-selling author, and mom of four

CHEF MELISSA D'ARABIAN is a go-to expert on affordable and healthy family home cooking. With an MBA from Georgetown University, Melissa enjoyed a successful career in corporate finance and strategy before becoming a stay-at-home mom. Passionate about sharing her tried-and-true recipes and money-saving tactics, Melissa then competed on and won season five of "Food Network Star." She soon became well known for Ten Dollar Dinners – her popular Food Network show and *New York Times* bestselling cookbook. Melissa's second cookbook, *Supermarket Healthy*, proves healthy eating can be easy, affordable and achievable with ingredients from the neighborhood grocery store.

Today, Melissa can also be found serving as a regular judge on the hit Food Network primetime series "Guy's Grocery Games," writing the nationally syndicated weekly "Healthy Plate" column for *The Associated Press*, and hosting multiple FoodNetwork.com series. A sought-after expert regularly featured in national media, Melissa shares her diverse life experiences and wide-ranging expertise on topics including food and cooking, money-saving strategies, family and parenting, healthy lifestyle, business and leadership, faith and causes close to her heart including suicide prevention and childhood hunger. She and her family live just outside San Diego.

//////

DESSERTS

Liz's Famous $1,000 Lemon Cookies H K

LIZ SCOTT, ALEX'S MOM

Liz bakes these cookies every year for The Lemon Ball Auction in Philadelphia to benefit Alex's Lemonade Stand Foundation. Each plate that is auctioned usually sells for about $1,000 a cookie. She was even on NBC's "Today" showing how she makes these cookies. Guests at the Lemon Ball look forward to her cookies every year.

MAKES ABOUT 3 DOZEN COOKIES

1 8 oz container Cool Whip topping, thawed but still cool
2 eggs
1 18.25 oz package lemon cake mix
⅓ cup confectioners' sugar for decoration

Preheat oven to 350 degrees and lightly grease baking sheets. Beat the Cool Whip and eggs together. Add the lemon cake mix and continue to mix. Dough will be thick.

Drop the dough by the teaspoonful into a bowl of confectioners' sugar and roll to coat.

Place cookies on the prepared baking sheets then bake for 8 minutes. Watch closely - they only have about 45 seconds between not being baked enough and being overdone!

Put on the fanciest plate of your choosing and no one will ever know how easy this recipe is!

Alex (age 8) and Liz Scott

LIZ SCOTT is Alex's mom and Co-Executive Director of Alex's Lemonade Stand Foundation, but she is most proud of her title of "Mom" to her three sons, Patrick, Eddie and Joey. Alex was diagnosed with neuroblastoma, a childhood cancer, when she was just an infant. In 2000, at 4 years-old, Alex announced that she wanted to hold a lemonade stand to raise money to help find a cure for other children with cancer. In her lifetime, Alex would go on to raise over $1 million before she passed away in 2004 at the age of 8. Since that time, Liz and her husband Jay have worked alongside thousands of supporters across the country to carry on her legacy of hope. While Liz doesn't consider herself talented in the kitchen, she does love to eat. In her free time, she enjoys hanging out with her family.

Limoncello Tiramisu

JEFF MICHAUD

A note from Chef Michaud: Tiramisu is like an Italian Tastykake (a beloved Philadelphia snack cake). You soak cookies in syrup and layer them between a creamy mascarpone filling. You can flavor the syrup and filling however you like. Coffee and chocolate are the most common combination, but my wife Claudia always made tiramisu with fruit that grew in her backyard in Italy. Her cherry tiramisu was one of my favorites. Then she came up with limoncello tiramisu. It's my new favorite. Refreshing, rich and ridiculously good.

MAKES 9" CAKE PAN

To make the mascarpone mousse:

8 large eggs
1 ½ cups granulated sugar
2 lb mascarpone (about 4 ¼ cups)
2 lemons

Separate the eggs, putting the yolks in a medium bowl and the whites in another bowl. Add 1 cup of the sugar to the yolks and whip with an electric mixer until thick and pale yellow in color, 2 to 3 minutes. Beat the mascarpone in a separate bowl with clean beaters until softened. Add the whipped yolks and beat until smooth. Grate the zest from the lemons and squeeze out ¼ cup lemon juice. Stir the lemon zest and juice into the mascarpone mixture.

Whip the egg whites in a clean bowl with clean beaters on medium speed until frothy, 2 to 3 minutes. Add the remaining ½ cup sugar and whip on medium-high speed until the whites form medium-soft peaks when the beaters are lifted, another 2 to 3 minutes.

Fold the whipped whites into the mascarpone mixture to form a mousse.

To make the limoncello-soaked ladyfingers:

¾ cup granulated sugar
1 ½ cups Pina's limoncello (in the Cocktails section) or other limoncello
1 package (about 8 oz) ladyfingers, about 30 ladyfingers

Combine the sugar and ¾ cup of water in a small saucepan over medium-high heat. Bring to a simmer and cook just until the sugar dissolves. Remove from the heat and set the pan in an ice bath to cool down the syrup. Stir in the limoncello.

Soak the ladyfingers in the limoncello syrup in batches for 20 seconds; the cookies should not be saturated all the way to the center. As you work, lay the soaked ladyfingers in the bottom of a 2 ½ quart baking dish, breaking up the cookies as necessary to make an even layer. Spread a layer of mousse over the ladyfingers. Continue making layers of soaked ladyfingers and mousse until the dish is filled, ending with a layer of mousse on top. Cover and refrigerate for at least 2 hours or up to 1 day.

Prep ahead:
The finished tiramisu can be refrigerated for up to 1 day before serving. It is ideal after just a few hours in the fridge, as the ladyfingers will continue to soak up liquid in the tiramisu and eventually become soggy.

Triple Berry Trifle H K

THE RICHARDSON FAMILY

A note from the Richardson family: On January 22, 2015, our precious 12-year-old daughter Peyton was diagnosed with high risk pre-B cell acute lymphoblastic leukemia. Our family was devastated. Peyton began treatment on January 23 and is currently in treatment for leukemia at Texas Children's Hospital.

We learned of Alex's Lemonade Stand Foundation, and we knew—Peyton knew—our family wanted to be involved with an organization whose greatest hope is to find a cure for childhood cancer. We enjoy cooking and baking together as a family, and this is one of our favorite go-to recipes.

SERVES 6 TO 8

Pound Cake (cubed)
1 cup of plain Greek yogurt
2 Tbsp honey
2 cups of strawberries (quartered)
2 cups of raspberries
2 cups of blueberries
1 Tbsp of mint (optional)

Start by cubing your pound cake. If you are using frozen pound cake, thaw first or you can also make your own. Next prepare the fruit. Rinse and quarter the strawberries. Rinse the raspberries and blueberries.

Make the yogurt sauce by mixing the Greek yogurt and honey until smooth.

For the trifle, take your trifle bowl and layer the bottom with pound cake. Next, add a layer of the yogurt sauce and then add the berries. Repeat until you reach the top. Add a sprig of mint on top for a little garnish.

When a child is diagnosed with cancer, the entire family is affected.

PEYTON RICHARDSON, who is battling high risk pre-B cell acute lymphoblastic leukemia, and her younger brother, Major, share a tight bond and are best friends. Major misses his sister when she is at the hospital for treatments, but he says, "I know she is getting better every day and that makes my heart happy."

Peyton was living life as a normal 12-year-old, cheering for the middle school football team, dancing with her ballet company and busy rehearsing for the Sugar Land production of "The Nutcracker." After her performance, Peyton started experiencing extreme fatigue. Her mother, Carrie, watched Peyton's ballet class in disbelief as she could not complete a combination across the floor. Carrie contacted their pediatrician immediately. Peyton had blood work done and was sent to the ER at Texas Children's Hospital. She was diagnosed with high-risk pre-B cell acute lymphoblastic leukemia and started chemotherapy the next day. Peyton has received a bone marrow biopsy, countless spinal taps and chemotherapy drugs. Peyton has not let her cancer diagnosis stop her from dancing. One of the first questions she asked was, "When can I go back to ballet?" Exactly two months after her diagnosis, Peyton danced across the ballet studio with the biggest smile. Peyton says ballet is harder than cancer and you'll understand why if you've ever danced with pointe shoes. Peyton is a shining example that through faith and determination, not even cancer can stand in your way. Peyton believes that through her own cancer diagnosis she can make difference in another child's life. She is making lemonade out of her lemons!

Peyton's brother, Major, is always happy from the minute he wakes up in the morning until he goes to sleep at night! Major loves school and his friends. He is truly a great friend, constantly encouraging his buddies, giving them high-fives and telling them "good job" on the playing field. Major's family describes him as the life of the party. Peyton's child life specialist first told their family about SuperSibs, a support program for the siblings of kids with childhood cancer. SuperSibs, powered by Alex's Lemonade Stand Foundation, sent Major a book and other resources specifically for him. He has never been jealous of the gifts Peyton has received since her diagnosis, but Major loved receiving the book about Jack who is also a sibling of a cancer patient. Major brought his book to school to read to his counselor. She later shared how much that book helped her because she understood that siblings of cancer patients are so much more affected than a lot of people realize. The Richardson's were one of 36 families chosen as a 2016 Lemonade Days Hero Representative, representing the number of children diagnosed with cancer every day in the United States.

UGHTERS
VE ME

Creamy Vanilla Bread Pudding

BARBARA LYNCH

A note from Chef Lynch: Rich and comforting, this is a signature dessert I make at the restaurant and when I entertain at home. It's simple to prepare and actually can taste better if made well in advance making it a perfect dish for taking to parties. If you do make it ahead of time, refrigerate, allow to come to room temperature, and serve gently warmed to really be able to taste the vanilla.

SERVES 8 TO 10

4 cups heavy cream
1 vanilla bean
¼ tsp kosher salt
5 cups cubed brioche
5 eggs
1 cup sugar
1 tsp good quality vanilla extract
2 cups Chantilly cream

Preheat the oven to 350 degrees.

Split vanilla bean length-wise. With the tip of a paring knife scrape the vanilla seeds out and add seeds and pod to heavy cream in a medium saucepan. Stir in the salt and heat until just below a simmer. Remove the pot from heat and allow the vanilla to steep for an hour.

In the meantime, place the brioche cubes in a 9" x 13" baking dish. In a medium bowl, whisk together the eggs and sugar until light yellow in color. Add vanilla extract.

Remove and discard the vanilla pod from the heavy cream. Reheat the heavy cream over medium high heat just until it comes to a simmer. Do not allow it to boil. Remove from the heat.

Temper the eggs by slowly pouring ⅓ of the hot cream into egg mixture, whisking constantly. Pour the egg-cream mixture into the saucepan with remaining cream and whisk together. Strain the custard through a fine mesh sieve over the bread cubes in the baking dish. Allow the brioche to absorb the custard for at least 30 minutes before baking.

Place the bread pudding dish in a larger roasting pan. Add enough hot water to the roaster until the water is halfway up the sides of the baking dish. Bake in the center of the oven until just firm, 50 minutes to 1 hour (begin checking earlier; give the pan a gentle shake and take it out of the oven when the custard is no longer jiggling). The bread pudding can be served warm, room temperature, or even cold. Serve with a dollop of Chantilly cream.

CHEF BARBARA LYNCH grew up in South Boston and by 13 she was working her first job at a local rectory kitchen. It took an influential home economics teacher and a gig at Boston's esteemed St. Botolph Club to put the teenage Lynch on a direct path to chefdom. Lynch earned acclaim at **Galleria**, but it was **No. 9 Park** that established her as a rock in the foundation of Boston gastronomy. Opening in 1998, No. 9 Park quickly became a breeding ground for Boston culinary talent and expression. An empire rapidly erupted, with Lynch opening **B&G Oysters**, **The Butcher Shop**, and **Stir** cookbook store and demo kitchen in the South End, followed by **Drink** cocktail bar, and **Sportello** in Fort Point. In that same neighborhood, Lynch opened crown jewel **Menton** in 2010, the only Relais & Chateaux property in Boston.

Not only is Chef Lynch the only woman in the United States who holds the title Grand Chef Relais & Chateaux, she's won a slew of James Beard Foundation Awards including "Best Chef: Northeast" 2007, induction into the "Who's Who of Food and Beverage in America" 2013, and "Outstanding Restaurateur" in 2014. A member of Women Chefs & Restaurateurs, Les Maîtres Cuisiniers and the Bocuse d'Or USA Culinary Council, Chef Lynch has made outreach and equality major tenets in the **Barbara Lynch Gruppo**. Her first cookbook, *Stir: Mixing It Up in the Italian Tradition*, is soon to be followed by a memoir. Meanwhile, the opening of The Barbara Lynch Foundation in 2012 has ensured that Chef Lynch can keep on giving back to the city she loves and loves to feed. Chef Lynch has been supporting Alex's Lemonade Stand Foundation since 2014, participating in L.A. Loves Alex's Lemonade and The Great Chefs Event.

Jim Jams K

KIRSTEN VANGSNESS

This recipe is one of Kristen's childhood favorites, passed down to her from her paternal grandmother, Oline. The cookies are buttery and chewy with a hint of vanilla that will instantly delight kids and adults alike.

MAKES 2 TO 3 DOZEN COOKIES

1 cup shortening
1 cup sugar
2 eggs
½ cup molasses
2 tsp cinnamon
½ tsp salt
2 tsp baking soda in 3 Tbsp warm water
1 tsp vanilla extract
3 ½ to 4 cups flour

Preheat the oven to 350 degrees.

Combine together all ingredients until they are just mixed.

Use a teaspoon to scoop out dough and place them on a cookie sheet, keeping the size small.

Bake for 9 minutes. Let rest for 1 minute on tray then transfer to wire racks.

Jim Jams can be frosted, but they taste great plain as well!

Actress and writer **KIRSTEN VANGSNESS** is best-known for her role as Penelope Garcia in CBS's "Criminal Minds." Born in Pasadena, California, Kirsten graduated from California State University and got her first big break in the theatre. She won several awards including "15 Minutes of Female Best Actress Award," the Los Angeles Drama Critics Award for "Best Emerging Comic Actress" and the "Golden Betty Award." Her work has been published in the *Los Angeles Times* and she has co-written several episodes of "Criminal Minds." Kirsten has been a big supporter of Alex's Lemonade Stand Foundation, serving on the Honorary Committee of L.A. Loves Alex's Lemonade. She has also been an outspoken supporter for the cause and has lent her voice to record several public service announcements in support of the Foundation.

Welch Cookies H K

THE LITTLEFIELD FAMILY

A note from hero mom, Kristen: Growing up, my grandma would wake up early to cook in peace—there was always a handful of grandkids around. Sometimes, my cousin and I would sleepover and we would wake up and cook with Grandma. Many mornings we would bake these rollout cookies with her. As a parent, I try to pass down the things I loved as a child to my children and this is one of them—we just don't wake up super early to cook these cookies, though! My daughter Lucy enjoys helping to make these cookies and loves to eat them. I'll even let her eat these cookies for breakfast!

4 cups flour (typically we add more to get the consistency we want once all ingredients are mixed)
1 ¾ cups sugar
2 tsp salt
3 tsp baking powder
3 tsp cinnamon
3 tsp nutmeg
2 sticks margarine
1 box of currants
3 eggs
1 tsp vanilla extract
Milk, as needed

Turn griddle on medium low, you cook these cookies on the stove top like you are making pancakes. Start this early on so that the temperature gets regulated on the surface.
Mix the flour, sugar, salt, baking powder, cinnamon, currants and nutmeg.

Blend in margarine as though you are making a pie crust.

In a measuring cup, add 3 beaten eggs, 1 tsp vanilla then add in milk until you are at 1 cup of wet ingredients.

Add the 1 cup of wet ingredients to the dry mixture. Mix this until it's the consistency of a pie crust. You may need to add more flour so it's not so wet and can roll out nicely
On a floured surface, roll out your dough (about ¼" to ½" thick), use the rim of a cup to cut the cookies out.

Start to cook your cookies on the griddle. Depending on the stove, they will cook for about 5 minutes per side. Flip once they are golden.

Cool and enjoy.

LUCY LITTLEFIELD was diagnosed with neuroblastoma, stage 4 low risk, at 11-weeks-old in April of 2009. She was under watchful eyes for a few weeks until the doctors decided to do two rounds of chemotherapy to shrink her tumor faster. After the chemotherapy, her tumor shrank more than 50%. A few weeks later (and 7 months after diagnosis) Lucy had another set of scans showing that her tumor was no longer there! As of September 2016, Lucy celebrates 7 years cancer free.

Lucy is a creative, fun loving, second grader. She loves all things art, playing with her three younger sisters and her friends, she enjoys going to the beach and does well in school. Lucy also enjoys hosting her annual Alex's Lemonade Stand. Team Little Lucy has raised thousands of dollars through the Lemon Run and other events to fight childhood cancer.

Red Rooster Donuts

MARCUS SAMUELSSON

A note from Chef Samuelsson: New York City's donut scene has never been more vibrant. Conventionally a decadent breakfast treat, donuts now regularly appear on dessert menus. In New York City, restaurants serve up donuts that range from traditional to bizarre. But whatever form they take, donuts add a bit of whimsy to any meal.

SERVES 10

To make the donuts:

1 cup water
1 ½ tsp fresh yeast
1 cup sugar
3 ½ cup bread flour
1 tsp salt
5 eggs
1 tsp vanilla paste
1 cup cold butter, cubed

In a stand mixer with the hook attachment, stir together warm water, yeast, sugar, flour and salt. Let sit for 5 minutes.

Add eggs and stir for 15 minutes.

Beat in butter and vanilla for 15 to 20 minutes, or until glossy.

Remove bowl from electric mixer, cover with a towel and let it sit in a warm area for one hour.

Place dough onto a cold surface and roll until ½" thick.

Using 1" diameter circular cutters, cut donuts out of dough and let sit until double in size.

Meanwhile heat oil to 375 degrees in a large pot.

Fry donuts until brown on all sides, about 5 minutes.

To make the filling:

1 ½ cup milk
3 yolks
¼ cup sugar
4 Tbsp cornstarch
1 pinch salt
1 cup sweet potato puree
2 Tbsp brown sugar
1 tsp vanilla extract
¼ tsp cinnamon

In a small bowl, combine sugar, yolks, salt and cornstarch.

Place milk in a pot over medium heat and bring to a boil. Once boiling, pour over yolk mixture and whisk together then pour back into pot.

Turn heat to medium and cook until boiling.

In a food processor, mix together sweet potato, brown sugar, cinnamon and vanilla for 15 minutes or until smooth.

Stuff fried donuts with sweet potato cream filling and roll in cinnamon sugar. If desired, serve with a side of whipped cream.

Award-winning chef, restauranteur, author and TV personality

CHEF MARCUS SAMUELSSON is the acclaimed chef behind **Red Rooster Harlem**, **Ginny's Supper Club**, **Streetbird Rotisserie** and **Marcus National Harbor**. A committed philanthropist and the youngest person to ever receive a three-star review from *The New York Times*, Samuelsson has won multiple James Beard Foundation Awards including "Best Chef: New York City," and was tasked with planning and executing the Obama Administration's first state dinner. Samuelsson was also crowned champion of television shows "Top Chef Masters" and "Chopped All Stars," and served as a mentor on ABC's "The Taste." Samuelsson co-produced Harlem EatUp!, a food and culture festival launched in Harlem, New York in 2015, and he is also the founder of the website Food Republic. He is the author of *The New York Times* best-selling memoir *Yes, Chef*, the young adult version, *Make It Messy*, *Marcus Off Duty* and his newest cookbook, *The Red Rooster Cookbook: The Story of Food and Hustle in Harlem.* In 2016, he was inducted into the James Beard Foundation's *Who's Who of Food and Beverage in America.*

Chef Samuelsson has been a supporter of Alex's Lemonade Stand Foundation since 2011 participating as a chef at the annual Lemon: NYC culinary event.

Brown Bag Apple Pie H K

TAYLOR HAY

Brown paper bag pie recipes have been passed down from generation to generation and are used by some of the country's best apple pie bakers. The bag helps cook the apples without over baking or browning, while sealing in all of the juicy flavors. Plus, the mess stays in the bag and your oven stays clean. But whatever you do, don't peek inside the bag until it's done cooking!

1 pre-made or homemade deep dish pie crust
5 to 6 Granny Smith apples
¾ cup granulated sugar
2 Tbsp all-purpose flour
A dash of cinnamon
2 tsp fresh or bottled lemon juice
½ cup granulated sugar
½ cup all-purpose flour
½ cup salted butter

Pre-heat oven to 400 degrees.

Cut apples into chunks about the size of the end of your thumb. In a medium-sized bowl, mix sugar, flour and cinnamon. Toss apple chunks in the flour and sugar mixture. Pour the apple chunks into the pie crust. Sprinkle with the lemon juice. In a separate bowl, cream butter until smooth. Mix sugar, flour and butter with a pastry cutter until the mixture forms small, pebble-sized chunks. Using your palms, pat spoonfuls of the topping mixture into flat sections and arrange on the top of the pie to form a loose crust.

Insert pie into a brown paper grocery store bag, making sure the top is tented and not touching the top of the pie. Fold the open end, close and staple to secure. Holding one end of the bag and using a small, sharp knife, cut vent slits into the paper bag over the top of the crust. Adjust wire rack inside the oven down to allow the pie to sit on the rack without the paper bag touching the oven element. Gently place pie inside the bag into the oven, checking to be sure there is at least 1" to 2" clearance between the bag and the heating element. Bake for 60 to 75 minutes, just until the top crust turns golden. Remove from oven and let stand for five minutes before removing the paper bag. Allow to cool to room temperature or serve when slightly warm with whipped cream or ice cream if desired.

TAYLOR HAY has been working in the entertainment industry since she was 4-years-old. She started in commercials, then progressed to feature films before being stricken with non-Hodgkins lymphoma at the age of nine. Upon her recovery, she returned to the entertainment field and has worked on such films as the holiday special, "Yes, Virginia," animated by Tim Burton as well as the feature film, "Hellstorm." She was also seen as one of the new faces of Neutrogena's "Beautiful Because" national campaign and in Audi's Christmas commercial, "The Forecast." On the smaller screen, she recently appeared in the hit YouTube Red show, "Escape the Night," and the new horror series, "Strings."

As a model, she has worked with top couture designers and has walked the runways at both Los Angeles and San Diego Fashion Weeks and PopCon. Because of her bout with cancer, Taylor feels that giving back is important for each and every person. To do her part, not only has she volunteered her time with a wide variety of charities, she also founded Star for a Night in 2012, and hosts this annual charity event honoring young cancer patients and survivors that raises thousands of dollars for a variety of charities. In 2016, the event benefited Alex's Lemonade Stand Foundation. Since her remission, Taylor has helped raise over $1 million for charity.

Chewy Chocolatey Ice Cream Cookie Sandwiches K

ALEX GUARNASCHELLI

A note from Chef Guarnaschelli: These cookies have slight brownie qualities and, for that reason, I like to eat them on their own as much as when they are part of an ice cream sandwich. They are thin and chewy and chocolatey. After the cookies are baked and cooled, soften the ice cream and mold it with a spoon so it's ready to be sandwiched between two cookies. Pressing the cookies to make the ice cream behave will only break them and make messy sandwiches. These can be made and devoured on the spot (my favorite way to do it) or premade, wrapped in wax paper or foil and returned to the freezer for an old-fashioned homemade ice cream sandwich. My favorite flavors of ice cream to use? Butter pecan, vanilla, coffee and strawberry. I love to roll the sides in various toppings as well, from salted, roasted nuts to dried fruits or chopped pieces of chocolate. Do what you like!

MAKES 9 COOKIE SANDWICHES

Preheat the oven to 350 degrees. Grease 2 baking sheets with butter.

To melt the chocolate and butter:

2½ oz semisweet chocolate, roughly chopped (heaping ½ cup)
1½ oz unsweetened chocolate, roughly chopped (about ⅓ cup) cut into pieces
3 Tbsp lightly salted butter, plus more for the pan

In a medium bowl, combine the two kinds of chocolate and the butter. Create a makeshift double boiler by filling a pot that will hold the bowl snugly with 1" of water (the bowl should not touch the water). Bring the water to a boil. Lower the heat so the water is hot but not boiling. Keep the bowl there, stirring with a heatproof spatula from time to time, until the chocolate and butter melt. Remove from the heat.

To make the batter:

1 large egg
⅓ cup sugar
1 tsp vanilla extract
1 Tbsp plus 2 tsp all-purpose flour
⅛ tsp baking powder
¼ tsp kosher salt

In the bowl of an electric mixer fitted with the whisk attachment, beat the egg on high speed for 1 minute. Add the sugar and vanilla and beat until the mixture thickens slightly and becomes a pale yellow color, 3 to 5 minutes. Scrape down the sides of the bowl and add the chocolate mixture.

Sift together the flour and baking powder and stir into the chocolate. With a rubber spatula, stir in the salt. Slowly add the flour mixture to the chocolate mixture and stir until all of the ingredients are blended.

To bake the cookies:

Drop 1 Tbsp lumps of the cookie batter onto the baking sheets, leaving about 1½" between the cookies; they will spread as they cook. You should have about 18 cookies total, 9 per baking sheet. Bake for 4 minutes, rotate the pan from front to back, and bake until they spread and crack slightly, an additional 4 minutes. Let the cookies cool for 10 to 15 minutes on the pan before transferring them to a rack to cool completely.

To assemble the sandwiches:

1 pint ice cream

Molding the ice cream is key. I like to scoop a heaping tablespoonful or two, depending on the size and shape of the cookies, and press it into a fairly round 2"-thick shape. Then, sandwich it between 2 cookies and press gently. Repeat to fill all of the cookies.

Warm Chocolate Pudding Cake with Mascarpone Cream

MIRO USKOKOVIC

A note from Chef Uskokovic: My chocolate pudding cake is like a cross between lava cake and tiramisu, however the pudding part is darker and much more intense than lava cake. For a balance of flavor and creamy texture, we added light mascarpone cream that was flavored with condensed milk.

SERVES 4

To make the pudding cake:

10 ¼ oz 70% chocolate
10 ¼ oz unsalted butter + extra for ramekins
7 oz (about 4 large) whole eggs
3 oz (about 4 large) egg yolks
4 ½ oz organic sugar
Generous pinch of kosher salt
1 oz sorghum or buckwheat flour

Melt chocolate and butter together over double boiler, set aside to cool down. In a mixing bowl, combine eggs, yolks, sugar and salt and whisk until becomes frothy, but still liquid. Fold eggs into chocolate mixture. Add sorghum or buckwheat flour and mix to combine. Divide evenly between well buttered eight 8 oz. ramekins, filling only ½ way up.

Preheat oven on 400 degrees. Bake cakes for 7 minutes. Cake will still be molten in the middle. Remove from oven and let it sit for 5 minutes.

To make the mascarpone cream:

5 oz mascarpone cream
6 oz heavy cream
Pinch of kosher salt
5 oz condensed milk

Place all of the ingredients in a bowl of a stand mixer and whip until medium peaks form.

To assemble the dish:

Invert warm chocolate pudding cake on desired plate or bowl, top with mascarpone cream and garnish with cacao nibs and small malt chocolate balls, preferably Valrhona brand. You can additionally garnish with some extra grated 70% chocolate.

CHEF MIRO USKOKOVIC is the Pastry Chef of **Untitled** and **Gramercy Tavern**. Born and raised in Serbia, Miro grew up on a family farm where his mother had a small cheese and cake-making operation. After completing his program at the Culinary Institute of America, he went to **Jean Georges** as a pastry cook. Within a year and a half, Miro had become the Pastry Sous Chef at Jean Georges, working first under Johnny Iuzzini and then Pastry Chef Joseph Murphy. After several years at Jean Georges, Miro was named the Pastry Chef at **Aldea**, Chef George Mendes' Flatiron restaurant. Miro's contemporary American desserts are created out of a collection of personal memories and experiences, as well as influence from other cuisines. In 2014, Miro was named Pastry Chef at Gramercy Tavern before assuming the same role at **Untitled** and **Studio Cafe** at the Whitney Museum in 2015. Chef Uskokovic has participated in several Lemon: NYC events for Alex's Lemonade Stand Foundation.

Judi Bumstead's Famous Lemon Bars H K

GRACE BUMSTEAD

One of Grace's favorite treats is her grandmother's lemon bars. Grace dreams of being a mermaid. And a cook. And a waitress. And a ninja. And sometimes she wants to be a ninja that cooks while underwater.

2 cups sifted flour
½ cup powdered sugar
1 cup butter
¼ cup all-purpose flour
4 beaten eggs
2 cups granulated sugar
½ cup (plus 1 to 2 tsp as needed) fresh lemon juice
½ Tbsp baking powder

Sift together 2 cups flour and powdered sugar, cut in butter until mixture clings together. Press into 13" x 9" x 2" glass baking pan. Bake at 350 degrees for 20 to 25 minutes or until lightly brown.

Beat together eggs, sugar and lemon juice. Sift together the ¼ cup flour and ½ tsp baking powder. Stir in egg mixture. Pour over baked crust.

Bake at 350 degrees for 20 minutes more. Sprinkle with additional powdered sugar. Cool. Cut into bars. Store leftovers (if there are any!) in the fridge.

Her family calls **GRACE BUMSTEAD** their "Ninja Princess" because she loves to karate chop her cancer! Grace is rambunctious, tenacious, spunky and curious. She loves swimming, playing with friends, playing with dolls, dressing up and dancing like a princess (when she's not being a ninja).

Just a few weeks after Grace's fourth birthday, her mom started to notice abnormal bruising. Grace's pediatrician said it was because Grace was so active. Within a week, Grace got a giant purple bruise down her side. Her parents took her back to her doctor for blood work. That weekend, her parents got a terrible phone call: "I'm so sorry to tell you this over the phone, but Grace has every symptom of leukemia. You need to take her to the ER immediately."

They went to the local ER and were transferred to Children's Hospital Los Angeles (CHLA) by ambulance at midnight. Grace was in good spirits, chatting and flirting with the EMTs and telling them that she was a ninja in training.

Tests showed that Grace had a genetic mutation on her cancer cells, the Philadelphia chromosome, that made her cancer replicate rapidly and resist chemotherapy. Thankfully, Grace was able to immediately enroll in a clinical trial for the medicine, dasatinib, to counteract the genetic mutation in her cancer. She was also put on a high-risk protocol of very strong chemotherapy.

She spent over 100 days living at CHLA and she had several sets of high doses of chemotherapy. She suffered many side effects, which, while fortunately not life-threatening, were very painful. She had severe mucositis, nerve neuropathy and severe constipation that required hospitalization. In January of 2016, Grace finished treatment and is cancer free. She has started 1st grade and loves it, though adjusting to life outside the hospital was initially difficult. She counts riding a bike as a very big and recent accomplishment.

Grace's cancer journey has revealed not only her strength but also her compassion. Grace is always scanning the hospital to see if there are other kids who are afraid. She goes to them, explains her port access and tries to cheer them up if they're sad.

"I'M A NINJA. I PRACTICE EVERY DAY."

Jumbo Dinosaur Eggs filled with Nutella K

HEDY GOLDSMITH

A note from Chef Goldsmith: My inspiration for this dessert came about while working in Grand Cayman. Kids were everywhere you turned and I wanted to come up with a fun, almost silly dessert that was both gluten-free and peanut-free. Meringue and Nutella, like two peas in a pod—they really play well together. The kids love using the back of a spoon, cracking the "egg" and seeing the Nutella cream inside. The meringue stays soft inside like marshmallow cream. If you want to store them for the following day, don't fill them or they will start to get soggy. Store them in an odor-free airtight container at room temperature.

SERVES 12 KIDS

4 egg whites, at room temperature
1 cup extra-fine sugar
2 tsp cornstarch
1 tsp white vinegar
2 tsp pure vanilla extract (or 1 tsp vanilla bean paste)
Nutella or prepared pudding, for the filling

Heat the oven to 250 degrees. Line two sheet pans with parchment or silicone backing mats.

In a stand mixer fitted with the whip attachment, beat the egg whites on low to medium-low speed until they form soft peaks, 2 to 3 minutes. Increase the speed and very slowly add the sugar, 1 tsp. at a time. Beat until the mixture is glossy and thick; it will resemble marshmallow cream.

Remove the bowl from the mixer and scrape the whip. Sift the cornstarch over the meringue, add the vinegar and vanilla and gently fold until everything is incorporated. (Cocoa nibs, chia seeds, flax or even basil seeds can also be folded into the meringue.)

With a very large spoon, dip the spoon, into warm water, drain and scoop into the meringue. The shape of the spoon is oval, so when you place the meringue on the sheet pan, it resembles a jumbo egg. Continue scooping, rinsing the spoon after every scoop (which helps the eggs keep their proper shape and makes for much neater, smooth meringue).

(continued)

Put the eggs in the oven (if you have a convection oven, set it to 225 degrees). Keep it in the oven for at least 90 minutes. If they start to slightly change color, lower the oven by at least 25 degrees. Don't rush meringue. It takes time to dry out enough so they can be easily lifted off the pan. When in doubt, leave them in longer. When properly baked, they will be very light and lift off the pan very easily. Turn off the oven; don't open the door. Let them cool slowly in the oven for about 30 to 40 minutes. Remove the pans from the cool oven. They're ready to be filled when totally cool inside.

Flip each egg over and, with a melon baller, make a hole just large enough for the tip of a piping bag to fit. Fill a piping bag with Nutella or chocolate pudding (or vanilla or butterscotch pudding; any flavor that your kids will like). For adults, fill the eggs with rich lemon curd, salted caramel or pastry cream. Squeeze the filling into the egg just until you can see that it's starting to come out. Flip the egg onto a serving platter. Instant birthday party!

After a storied career sweetening and revolutionizing the Miami culinary scene with her signature, retro-modern desserts at the empire she helped create with Chef Michael Schwartz, pastry **CHEF HEDY GOLDSMITH** relocated to Los Angeles, where she is launching three product lines under her Sweet Hedy baked goods line. A 2012 and 2013 James Beard Foundation Award finalist for the nationally-contested "Outstanding Pastry Chef" category, Goldsmith's first cookbook, *Baking Out Loud: Fun Desserts with Big Flavors*, was released in 2012. The media's hunger for Goldsmith and her desserts is insatiable with coverage on NBC's "Today" and Food Network, *The New York Times*, *PEOPLE* magazine, *The Wall Street Journal*, *Wine Spectator*, *Food & Wine* magazine and more. She and an all-star team of women defeated Bobby Flay on Food Network's "Iron Chef America" as the first all-female competitors. Goldsmith is in her sixth season on Cooking Channel's "Unique Sweets", creates seasonal recipes for CookingChannel.com and blogs about all things sweet on FoodNetwork.com.

Chef Goldsmith has been a supporter of Alex's Lemonade Stand Foundation by participating in the L.A. Loves Alex's Lemonade event since 2010 and Lemon: NYC. She says, "Baking is my passion! I have been so fortunate in my career that I want to give back to a community that has supported me. Chefs by nature want to please without asking much in return. Liz and Jay Scott are dedicated to realizing Alex's dream of eradicating childhood cancer. I am honored to be part of this important Foundation. This recipe is dedicated to Alex for she is our collective hero."

Bianco's Carrara Rice Cake (Lemony Rice Cake)

CHRIS BIANCO

This sunny cake has been passed down for generations through Chris' family. The "torta di riso" came from Chris' great-grandmother in Carrara, Italy, who handed it to her son in the Bronx, who passed it to his daughter, Francesca (Chris' Mom), who then baked it for her son Chris when he was a boy.

SERVES 8 TO 10

1 qt whole milk
½ vanilla bean
¼ tsp vanilla extract or paste
Rind and juice of 1 lemon or orange
1 ¼ cup Arborio or Anson Mills Carolina rice
1 ⅓ cups granulated sugar
8 large eggs
⅔ cup amaretto or limoncello, or ½ cup added lemon juice

Preheat the oven to 350 degrees. Grease and line a 9" spring form or loose-bottomed cake pan.

Place the milk, scraped vanilla bean, lemon rind and 1 cup sugar in a large saucepan and bring to a boil. Reduce the heat, add the rice and simmer over medium to low heat for 20 to 25 minutes, until the rice is al dente but the mixture has a creamy consistency. Remove from the heat and allow to cool. Discard the vanilla bean pod and lemon rind.

In a stand mixer with a whisk attachment, beat the eggs, remaining sugar, vanilla extract and lemon juice for 12 minutes, starting at a slow speed until the ingredients are combined and then increase to high speed.

Stir some of the egg mixture into the cooled rice to loosen it. Gently fold in the remainder of the egg mixture to form a smooth batter. Add the liqueur or lemon juice and mix well.

Pour the batter into the prepared pan and bake for one hour, until the top is light golden and set.

When **CHEF CHRIS BIANCO** started the diminutive **Pizzeria Bianco** inside the back corner of a neighborhood grocery store, little did he know that he would be such a driving force in the slow food movement and specifically the artisanal pizza front. Chris, who won the James Beard Foundation Award for "Best Chef: Southwest" in 2003, helped spawn a generation of independent and artisanal pizzerias, lending his advice, wisdom and food philosophies to dozens of fellow chefs and restaurateurs. For years, it has been a common sight to find lines forming at the Pizzeria early in the afternoon, with foodies from all over and locals alike queuing up in anticipation of getting a table and enjoying what has been called the best pizza in America. Now there is **Pane Bianco**, also in Phoenix, as well as two Pizzeria Bianco's in Arizona.

Chris' excellence and commitment to the culinary arts has been recognized by many, including Pizzeria Bianco nominated for a James Beard Foundation Award in the "Outstanding Restaurant" category (2013, 2014), *Thrillist* listed Pizzeria Bianco #1 for Arizona in its "Best of America" by state, *Zagat* named Chris as 1 of 6 chefs who changed pizza during the last 100+ years (2013), *The New York Times* called the pizza "perhaps the best in America" (2004) and *Food & Wine* labeled Chris' pizza as "arguably the best pizza in America" (2005, 2009). Chef Bianco has supported Alex's Lemonade Stand Foundation for many years as a participating chef in L.A. Loves Alex's Lemonade and The Great Chefs Event.

ABOUT ALEX SCOTT

Alexandra "Alex" Scott was born to Liz and Jay Scott in Manchester, Connecticut on January 18, 1996, the second of four children. Shortly before her first birthday, Alex was diagnosed with neuroblastoma, a type of childhood cancer.

On her first birthday, the doctors informed Alex's parents that if she beat her cancer, it was doubtful that she would ever walk again. Just two weeks later, Alex slightly moved her leg at her parents' request to kick. This was the first indication of who she would turn out to be - a determined, courageous, confident and inspiring child with big dreams and big accomplishments.

By her second birthday, Alex was crawling and able to stand up with leg braces. She worked hard to gain strength and to learn how to walk. She appeared to be beating the odds, until the shattering discovery within the next year that her tumors had started growing again. In January of 2000, the day after her fourth birthday, Alex was in the hospital for another treatment and informed her mother, "When I get out of the hospital, I want to have a lemonade stand." She said she wanted to give the money to doctors to allow them to "help other kids, like they helped me." True to her word, she held her first lemonade stand later that year with the help of her older brother and raised an amazing $2,000 for "her hospital."

While bravely battling her own cancer, Alex and her family continued to hold yearly lemonade stands in her front yard to benefit childhood cancer research. News spread of the remarkable sick child dedicated to helping other sick children. People from all over the world, moved by her story, held their own lemonade stands and donated the proceeds to Alex and her cause.

In August of 2004, Alex passed away at the age of 8, knowing that, with the help of others, she had raised more than $1 million to help find a cure for the disease that took her life. Alex's family — including brothers Patrick, Eddie and Joey—and supporters around the world are committed to continuing her inspiring legacy through Alex's Lemonade Stand Foundation.

ABOUT ALEX'S LEMONADE STAND FOUNDATION

In 2004 when Alex passed away at the age of eight—her lemonade stand and inspiration had raised more than $1 million towards finding a cure for the disease that took her life. Alex's Lemonade Stand Foundation (ALSF) was started by her parents, Liz and Jay Scott, in 2005 to continue the work that Alex began. The mission is simple: to raise money and awareness for childhood cancer—especially research into new treatments and cures—and to encourage and empower others, especially children, to get involved and make a difference for children with cancer.

Since Alex set up her first lemonade stand in 2000, truly exemplifying the saying "When life hands you lemons, make lemonade," ALSF has raised over $100 million. This money has helped to fund cutting-edge research projects leading to better treatments and cures for childhood cancer.

Alex's Lemonade Stand Foundation is the living embodiment of Alex's spirit of determination and hope. Like Alex, we believe that every person can make a difference. Together, we can bring about a cure.

To learn more, donate or get involved, please visit AlexsLemonade.org.

♥

ABOUT ALEX'S LEMONADE STAND FOUNDATION CULINARY EVENTS

Chefs across the country donate their time, passion, talents and amazing food creations for one cause: finding a cure for childhood cancer.

Since 2006, culinary events have raised millions of dollars for research. Much like Alex and her lemonade stand, culinary events benefiting ALSF have grown in a grassroots way, with chefs and restaurateurs inspired to do more each year.

It all began in 2006 with The First Annual Great Chefs Event hosted by Chef Marc Vetri and his Vetri Family of Restaurants partner, Jeff Benjamin. That first event brought together eight local Philadelphia chefs and 100 guests. The event raised $50,000 and planted a seed in the culinary world. Chefs that attended The Great Chefs Event were inspired by the energy, the cause and the need for cures for childhood cancer. These chefs brought ALSF culinary events home to their own cities. Now, there are four unique culinary events benefitting ALSF.

THE GREAT CHEFS EVENT is held each June at the Urban Outfitters headquarters at the Philadelphia Navy Yard. Chefs from across the United States and all around the world join the best bars, wineries and craft breweries for an evening of eating, drinking and fundraising.

The **L.A. LOVES ALEX'S LEMONADE** culinary cookout, held each fall in Los Angeles, features over 100 chefs, mixologists and vintners. Since 2010, Chefs Suzanne Goin, David Lentz and business partner Caroline Styne have hosted world-renown chefs, shining stars in the entertainment world, families and food lovers at this unique outdoor, dine around event.

Founded in 2011 by Chef Jonathan Waxman and hosted by Chef Alex Guarnaschelli since 2015, **LEMON: NYC** is held each year in New York City and brings together a diverse roster of chefs from New York City, Washington, D.C., Philadelphia, Cleveland and across the country.

First held in 2014, **LEMON: CHICAGO** is hosted by local chefs Paul Kahan and Tony Mantuano and restaurateur Donnie Madia. Renowned chefs from across the country come together to prepare and serve signature dishes to guests.

/////////////////

Photo credit (clockwise from top left): Philip Gabriel Photography, Philip Gabriel Photography, Galdone's Photography, Getty Images, Galdone's Photography, Galdone's Photography, Angela Brown, Angela Brown and Getty Images.

GREAT CHEFS
CHEFS
Alex's Lemonade Stand
MOUNTAIN DUDE
DANIEL SHARP
JENN LOUIS
LEMON: CHICAGO

♥ ACKNOWLEDGEMENTS

Alex's Lemonade Stand Foundation would like to thank all those who have generously donated their time and knowledge to the creation of this cookbook.

Thank you to our talented photographer, Jason Varney, who put together an amazing team and kindly donated his resources and expertise to make this cookbook beautiful. Since his involvement with the cookbook, Jason has participated in other Alex's Lemonade Stand fundraising campaigns and is an avid supporter.

Thank you to Heads of State, who donated their creative talents to this cookbook. Jason Kernevich, Joanna Simon and their award-winning team gave visual direction and guidance to the book.

We want to also thank Robert Marzinksky and Jonathon Adams for donating their time and talent as food stylists and culinary experts. Additionally prop stylist Kristi Hunter donated her time and expertise to create beautiful gastronomic scenes.

Additionally, many thanks to Liz Thompson, owner and editor at House Style Editing, for donating her expertise and spending countless hours editing the book to ensure the recipes are clear, the words are powerful and the stories are inspiring.

Thank you to each and every chef, mixologist and supporter who donated a recipe or contributed in any way. We are so lucky to have such an amazing and talented group of supporters. These chefs create masterpieces and we are honored that they shared a bit of their art with us here and for their ongoing efforts to raise awareness and funds.

Finally, we would like to thank staff, board members and volunteers for their hard work and dedication putting this book together. We especially would like to thank the following staff members for their leadership on this project: Elizabeth Romaine, Jaime Horenstein, Abigail Seligsohn, Annie Korp, Elisa Heisman and Trish Adkins. When we decided to make a cookbook, we knew it would be a complex project but with help from the culinary community, we knew we could do it. Our team persisted because of our belief in the idea, Alex's legacy, and that this cookbook is another way to reach people and engage them about the importance of research.

The daily actions of our team members and supporters play an integral role in achieving the mission of the Foundation – curing all childhood cancers.

We hope that you enjoy this cookbook.

JASON VARNEY

Jason Varney is a Philadelphia-based food, travel and lifestyle photographer who has worked with everyone on the food chain from organic farmers to celebrity chefs. His work has garnered praise throughout Philadelphia's dining scene since 2007 and can be regularly seen appearing in the pages of major magazines. Jason travels the world on assignment but is just as happy shooting recipes at home in his studio. His body of work includes cookbooks, hospitality branding, feature stories and covers for national print editorial and advertising campaigns for local and global brands. varneyphoto.com